Quick Guide

INTERIOR & EXTERIOR
PAINTING

CREATIVE HOMEOWNER PRESS®

COPYRIGHT © 1994
CREATIVE HOMEOWNER PRESS®
A Division of Federal Marketing Corp.
Upper Saddle River, NJ

Quick Guide is a registered trademark of Creative Homeowner Press®

Manufactured in the United States of America

Editorial Director: David Schiff
Writers: Walter Jowers, Alexander Samuelson
Copy Editor: Kimberly Catanzarite
Art Director: Annie Jeon
Graphic Designer: Brian Demeduk
Illustrators: Baker Vail, Paul Schumm

Cover Design: Warren Ramezzana
Cover Illustrations: Brian Demeduk

Electronic Prepress: TBC Color Imaging, Inc.
Printed at: Banta Company

Current Printing (last digit)
10 9 8 7 6 5 4 3 2 1

Quick Guide: Interior & Exterior Painting
LC: 93-073999
ISBN: 1-880029-30-8 (Paper)

CREATIVE HOMEOWNER PRESS®
A Division of Federal Marketing Corp.
24 Park Way
Upper Saddle River, NJ 07458

CONTENTS

SAFETY FIRST

Though all the designs and methods in this book have been tested for safety, it is not possible to overstate the importance of using the safest construction methods possible. What follows are reminders; some do's and don'ts of basic carpentry. They are not substitutes for your own common sense.

- *Always* use caution, care, and good judgment when following the procedures described in this book.

- *Always* be sure that the electrical setup is safe; be sure that no circuit is overloaded, and that all power tools and electrical outlets are properly grounded. Do not use power tools in wet locations.

- *Always* read container labels on paints, solvents, and other products; provide ventilation, and observe all other warnings.

- *Always* read the tool manufacturer's instructions for using a tool, especially the warnings.

- *Always* use holders or pushers to work pieces shorter than 3 inches on a table saw or jointer. Avoid working short pieces if you can.

- *Always* remove the key from any drill chuck (portable or press) before starting the drill.

- *Always* pay deliberate attention to how a tool works so that you can avoid being injured.

- *Always* know the limitations of your tools. Do not try to force them to do what they were not designed to do.

- *Always* make sure that any adjustment is locked before proceeding. For example, always check the rip fence on a table saw or the bevel adjustment on a portable saw before starting to work.

- *Always* clamp small pieces firmly to a bench or other work surfaces when sawing or drilling.

- *Always* wear the appropriate rubber or work gloves when handling chemicals, heavy construction or when sanding.

- *Always* wear a disposable mask when working with odors, dusts or mists. Use a special respirator when working with toxic substances.

- *Always* wear eye protection, especially when using power tools or striking metal on metal or concrete; a chip can fly off, for example, when chiseling concrete.

- *Always* be aware that there is never time for your body's reflexes to save you from injury from a power tool in a dangerous situation; everything happens too fast. Be *alert!*

- *Always* keep your hands away from the business ends of blades, cutters and bits.

- *Always* hold a portable circular saw with both hands so that you will know where your hands are.

- *Always* use a drill with an auxiliary handle to control the torque when large size bits are used.

- *Always* check your local building codes when planning new construction. The codes are intended to protect public safety and should be observed to the letter.

- *Never* work with power tools when you are tired or under the influence of alcohol or drugs.

- *Never* cut very small pieces of wood or pipe. Whenever possible, cut small pieces off larger pieces.

- *Never* change a blade or a bit unless the power cord is unplugged. Do not depend on the switch being off; you might accidentally hit it.

- *Never* work in insufficient lighting.

- *Never* work while wearing loose clothing, hanging hair, open cuffs, or jewelry.

- *Never* work with dull tools. Have them sharpened, or learn how to sharpen them yourself.

- *Never* use a power tool on a workpiece that is not firmly supported or clamped.

- *Never* saw a workpiece that spans a large distance between horses without close support on either side of the kerf; the piece can bend, closing the kerf and jamming the blade, causing saw kickback.

- *Never* support a workpiece with your leg or other part of your body when sawing.

- *Never* carry sharp or pointed tools, such as utility knives, awls, or chisels in your pocket. If you want to carry tools, use a special-purpose tool belt with leather pockets and holders.

CHOOSING PAINT & TOOLS

Today's paint and painting tools are better and easier to use than ever before. Armed with the proper paint and tools, you'll be able to produce professional-looking results even if you have never painted before.

Choosing Interior Colors

Inside the house, color choice is a matter of following your own taste. Just keep in mind that dark colors make a room seem smaller than light colors.

Choose a color to set the mood in a room, make a room seem larger or smaller, or simply match the new furniture. The elements of a room give visual clues to what colors will work. In a kitchen with bright appliances and white countertops a soft cream color with a sheen will look good. A deep, formal red may work well in a dining room filled with dark wood, but the same color makes a small bathroom look like a cave. Often accessories will dictate a room's color. A color can be plucked from a favorite pattern on the curtains or to accent a prominent piece of artwork. A room may feature interesting molding that will be highlighted by a sharp contrast with the walls. Interior color schemes should reflect the "personality" of a room as well as expressing your personal taste.

If you have not been to a paint store lately you will notice that the methods for picking paint colors have changed. Not long ago, people relied upon paint charts to choose the colors that would look best on their walls. They took the charts home, studied them and tried to imagine how the colors would look in each room. These days, the process is made a lot easier by using a computer program. Color combinations are entered into the computer and moments later the results appear on a screen: All the paint colors you want to see neatly applied to sample situations stored in computer memory.

Matching Colors

Many paint stores have computer systems that match colors. You can take a flower, a piece of fabric, or even a paint chip to the paint store, and the computer can design a color that matches the sample. The sample must be at least one square inch in size.

Keep in mind that computer technology is very helpful, but it is not fool-proof. Veteran painters know that colors on paint sample chips may vary significantly from the color that ends up on the wall. Veteran computer users know that a computer monitor's glowing pixels are only a representation of pigment colors. No real-world surface looks exactly like the picture on a monitor.

Buying Samples

Designers know it is best to make final decisions about paint colors only after you have seen sample patches of the actual colors applied to the surfaces being painted. Buy quarts of the colors you think you want to use, and paint a section of wall and a section of trim side by side. Look at the interior colors in natural light and artificial light. Give yourself a day or two to get used to the colors. If you are happy with these colors, the quarts of paint you purchased do not go to waste. If you are not happy with those colors, at least you have only wasted a couple of quarts rather than all the time and money used to apply several gallons of paint you do not like.

Choosing Interior Color. Use the room decor and furnishings as a guide for the interior paint colors. The amount of sunlight, the type of molding, and the shape of the room all influence the perception of a color.

Choosing Exterior Color

Paint that is used outside the house is equally about protection and color. A good exterior paint job will keep your house well maintained and attractive for years. The priming, caulking and patching that are a part of the prep work are the first line of defense in protecting a house from the elements.

Effect of Color

Choosing the colors for your house is an endeavor not to be taken lightly. The effort and expense of a paint job make it important that the color scheme works in the environment and pleases you aesthetically. Used properly, color can increase the feeling of space, height, and depth of your house.

Color draws the eye to architectural details, or acts as a softening influence. Emphasizing horizontal elements, such as a belly band between stories, makes a house appear shorter. Emphasizing the horizontal element is a trademark of Frank Lloyd Wright and his Prairie-style architecture. Calling attention to vertical elements—such as the half-timbering in the gables of a Tudor house—creates the illusion of a taller house. Your overall color scheme goal should be to create a unity of the architectural elements where no single element dominates and the features of the house appear balanced.

When choosing house colors, personal preferences should be the ultimate influence, but there are also elements of design to consider. Just as interior colors affect the perceived size of a room, exterior colors will affect the perceived size of your whole house. Light colors will make your house seem larger; darker colors will make it appear more intimate. Depending on the location, light and dark colors can make your building stand out, or appear in harmony with its surroundings. In the past, Victorian designers (true innovators in house painting) would choose a darker paint when a house was exposed on a lot, and a very light shade when it was concealed within a knoll of trees or shrubs.

A high-contrast scheme holds the eye at each detail, and will make

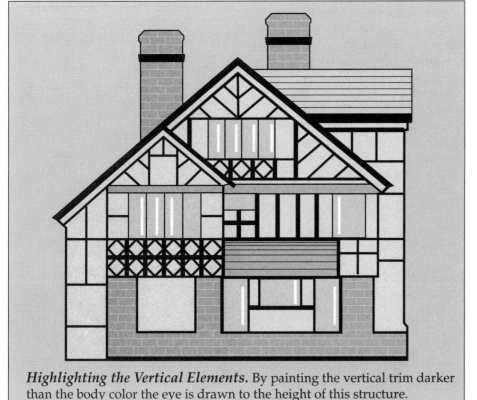

Highlighting the Vertical Elements. By painting the vertical trim darker than the body color the eye is drawn to the height of this structure.

Highlighting the Horizontal Elements. Color selection and placement emphasizes the horizontal elements of this home. A distinctive color on the fascia below the roofs will make the structure seem long and low.

your project appear smaller, while subtle contrast makes a surface seem unbroken and larger. Houses built with materials of different textures, such as stucco, brick and shingles, will appear to have fewer textures when painted one color. If you want to emphasize the difference in textures, paint each element a different color.

It's possible to enhance the effect of shadow by using light colors on projecting elements, and dark colors on the insets. Be careful when applying accents. Subtle changes in color and small detailed highlights will do more for your project than you might think.

How To Choose Colors

Two colors may work well together as a siding and trim combination, but when the job is finished may clash with the roof or look awful among other houses on the street. For these reasons it is important to look at colors as a whole scheme, both within a neighborhood and against each other on a single structure.

When deciding on a house color, consider the local customs in your town as well as your own tastes. Some towns insist upon this. For example, in the resort community of Hilton Head, South Carolina, residents must choose exterior colors from a limited palette of muted shades (even the stop signs have color restrictions).

And in the city of Charleston, there is a well-known district of pastel-colored houses called "Rainbow Row."

To work toward a final decision, take a walk through your neighborhood. Look at houses similar to yours, noting the colors and color combinations you like. Also, a great way to let experienced designers pick color combinations for you (without hiring an experienced designer) is to study the use of colors in fabric samples.

Color choice must factor in the givens—colors that you cannot or will not change. These may include the colors of the roofing material, the nearby landscape and plantings, any masonry work or perhaps your neighbors' houses. If your house has brick on the exterior, consider the brick color as well. (There is almost no good reason to paint brick, see page 42.) If you have a sample of roofing, or a piece of brick, use them along with color swatches to develop a color scheme.

It's also important to realize that if other elements are close enough, their reflected light can actually affect the way you perceive your chosen color.

Of course you can overdo your concern with the givens. For instance, during the Victorian period, some people tried to "blend" their homes into the landscape by copying the

"harmonious colors of nature" (soil, rocks, and wood) but often the result was dirty yellow houses that seemed to spring up out of the mud.

You can start deciding on color placement without actually using paint. Trace or sketch a line drawing of your house and then make several photocopies to try different schemes. Using a pencil, try shading different features to experiment with highlighting possibilities. Decide which features you would like to emphasize and which ones you would like to hide. The different degrees of shading will later correspond with appropriate colors. The goal here is to create a well-balanced whole where no element seems to dominate. By "prepainting" in this manner, you will not only avoid any disappointment, but it will also encourage you to try to some distinctive schemes before you pick up the paintbrush.

Again, some paint stores feature computers that will "paint" your house for you right on the computer screen. The better systems are equipped to scan a high contrast photo of your home; others have preprogrammed home styles. Even if you are unable to get an exact reproduction of your house, these programs will give you a sense of what sorts of combinations are pleasing and demonstrate some ideas of how you might paint.

How Light Affects Plants

Plant growth depends partly on the color of the light they receive. Although it's not as important as good gardening, your choice of color will affect the spectrum that your plants receive:

White produces a balanced growth between foliage and flower but can reflect too much light. Care should be taken to ensure that the plants do not dry out.

Yellow and Green have no noticeable effect

Blue and Violet cause foliage to be darker green

Red helps produce more, bigger and brighter flowers

Black slows growth by absorbing light.

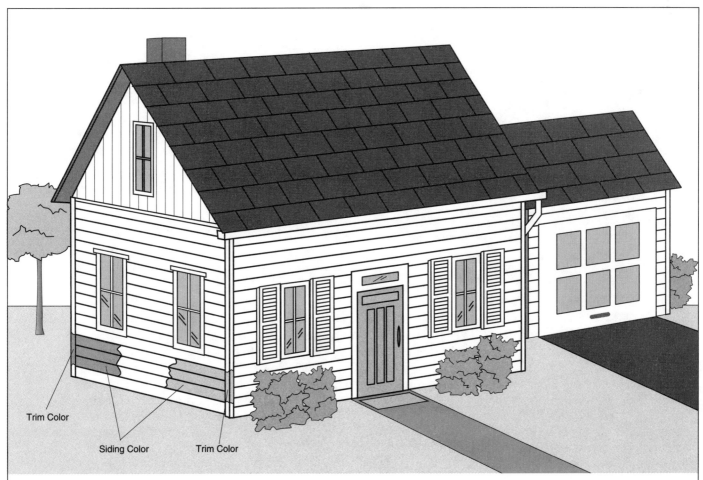

Trim Color

Siding Color   Trim Color

Painting Sample Colors. Paint a swatch of the siding and the trim color next to one another as they willl appear on the structure.

Testing Color

Everyone knows what white looks like, but if you decide to use something a little different, you should invest the time in testing that choice to make sure it's the color that you think it is. Remember that perceived color is affected by several factors:

Colors look different in different types of light. What you thought was a wonderful pink under the fluorescent lights of the paint store, may appear too pale or even garish in sunlight. The best place to compare colors is outside, preferably on a shady, or overcast day. That way you'll be able to study the color under the full spectrum of light, but without worrying about glare.

Color is affected by the colors next to it. Remember that same pink? It might make a wonderful contrast

to the blue trim, but it could also clash horribly with the pine trees in the yard.

How much there is of a color affects how you see it. It is possible to have too much of a good thing. What looks fine on a can lid may not look as becoming on your entire house. We perceive colors to intensify with size.

Using Color Chips & Samples

The first thing you should do before selecting any color from a chip is to isolate it from the other colors on that card. Cut out a small frame of white paper to expose just one color value at a time. When you are starting to select color scheme combinations, try framing them against a white background, and then against a black background to help bring out the various undertones in the different colors.

Most professional color designers will not pick colors from chips. Chips are too small to adequately show the impact that the color will have on a large project. As with interior paint choices, you can avoid later disappointment by purchasing quart-size cans of paint and testing the colors on a scrap board or inconspicuous part of the house (this is called swatching). Paint large swatches, and be sure that the colors that will be used together are located next to each other on your test. Try to swatch roughly the same percentages of paints that will be used on the house. In other words, if about 90 percent of the your house is clapboards with the rest trim, paint a large swatch of the clapboard color next to a small swatch of trim color. Note the colors at different times of the day since different levels of sunlight will also

Roof/Trim/Siding Combinations. Dark colors make a house seem smaller (left) while light colors make it seem larger (right). Contrasting colors in a paint scheme highlight features and define shapes.

affect how a color "reads". Remember also that the colors will darken as the paint dries. It's a good idea to look at your house from a distance so that you can get some idea of how the color scheme will work in with the rest of the yard.

Painting: What Goes Where

Now that you have selected the colors for your home, it's time to decide which colors should be assigned to specific architectural elements. Generally the siding is done in one color, but if there is decorative molding above the first floor, a second color siding can be very interesting. Casings around windows and doors should be the same color or the house will seem too busy. If there is decorative highlights in your trim and molding, two or more colors are fine if the pattern repeats on the whole structure.

The current fashion is to paint the window sash and trim a color that is lighter than the body of the house. Shutters, if present, are usually painted darker than the house body. Of course, fashions change. For example, at the turn of the century gloss black was the most popular choice for the window sash, but except for shutters, you do not see much gloss black on houses these days.

Here's some tips for other architectural highlights:

Front Entrance. Create a striking effect by breaking out this important element of your home. For example, a white house with a door painted a bright color, such as red or green, draws attention to the door, making the entrance seem more inviting.

Frieze. A historically appropriate treatment for the frieze is to use both

Pre-fab Color Schemes

Deciding on the specific colors in a multi-color scheme is a little tricky. It's for that reason that almost all of the major paint companies have created "combo cards" to help you to pick base and trim colors in one step. These colors are also available in historic shades designed to match the most prevalent color schemes of certain periods. One nice feature of these cards is that the trim and accent color chips often overlap the body color, which helps demonstrate a more realistic relationship.

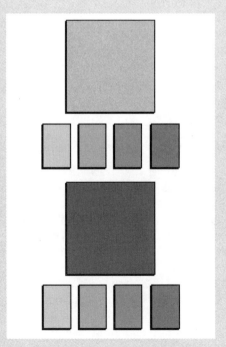

Architectural Highlights. Make your paint scheme more interesting with contrasting or complementary colors on the various architectural details such as the frieze, corner brackets, railings and posts.

the trim and body colors. Let the trim color be the dominate one to mark a clear distinction from the top of the siding. Be careful not to introduce too many colors though, you could end up with an effect that is too busy.

Corner Brackets. Brackets need to be perceived as part of the overall structure, and should be painted so as not to appear that they are "floating free" of the structure. Use the principal trim color. Avoid using too much color. Some painters add a leading edge of scarlet to these features. Sandwich brackets are a little different. Because they consist of more than one layer and are more complex than simple corner brack-

ets, it is more acceptable to use several colors. Paint the exterior pieces to match the trim and frieze, and the center another color to show off your scroll work.

Posts. If you have simple rectangular wooden posts on a porch you probably don't want to emphasize them with their own color. Paint them to match either the overall trim or body paint of your house. However, if your posts have special millwork, such as a chamfer on a square post or a ring on a turned post, it is perfectly acceptable to highlight these decorations with a flourish.

Rails. The rails are essentially extensions of the posts. Therefore,

they are usually painted in the same color as the posts.

Balusters. Try painting the balusters a lighter color than the rails. If the posts and rails have been treated in the main body color, try using the trim colors to make them stand out. Even if you have elaborately worked balusters, don't use too many colors to demonstrate your handiwork. Besides the amount of time that would be involved in detailing each baluster, the effect will look busy.

Floors and Ceiling. Porches are painted certain colors not only for decoration, but as matters of practicality. Light colored ceilings maintain a sense of airness and brightness. Painting porch ceilings blue is a technique that has been used for centuries to suggest the sky overhead and is rumored to repel insects. If the undersides of your porch ceiling rafters are exposed, you might paint them by using a combination of the body and trim colors. A dark floor is even more practical because it shows dirt and tracks less readily than a floor painted a lighter color.

Steps and Risers. The risers of wooden steps are normally painted the trim color, while the treads carry a surface (porch or deck) to the ground and should be painted in the same color. The handrail and balusters on the steps should be painted to match the porch rail and baluster color scheme.

Masonry Foundations. Many houses have a band of brick or concrete block below the siding. While it is fine to have this band the same color as the siding, a darker color makes the house seem firmly planted and will hide dirt and mud. Basement windows are generally painted the same dark color to de-emphasize them.

Buying Paint

The first rule of buying paint is: Never buy cheap paint because it is never good. Among top-of-the-line paints, there are variations in quality. Reputable paint suppliers usually sell top-of-the-line paint that is very good. One way to save money on brand-name paint is to buy premixed standard colors. They are less expensive than colors that have to be mixed at the store.

Read the can labels to compare paint ingredients. And remember, the heavier the can, the better the paint.

Latex Versus Oil-Based Paints

Paint is composed of pigment, a vehicle, solvents and additives, all of which affect the flow and drying

characteristics of the paint. With latex paint, the vehicle is a water-based emulsion. With oil-based paint, the vehicle is natural or synthetic (alkyd) oil. A third, new type of paint is latex paint that has some alkyd resins.

Choosing Latex Paint. Homeowners and professional painters like latex paint because it dries in just a few hours and because cleanup is easy. Quick drying allows the application of two coats in one day. When the job is done, everything can be cleaned with soap and warm water.

Latex paint is environmentally friendlier than its oil-based cousin. Unlike oil-based paint, latex does not emit volatile organic compounds (VOCs), which have been virtually outlawed in some states. Also latex paint does not require toxic solvents such as mineral spirits for cleanup. Compared to oil-based paint, latex paint is easier on the eyes, nose, lungs and skin.

In the past, however, many professional painters have resisted using latex paint. They preferred oil-based

paint, especially for woodwork and areas where the paint has to hold up to a lot of scrubbing, such as the kitchen and bathroom. The truth was, that even the best latex enamel did not dry quite as hard, smooth or shiny as a good oil-based paint. Some painters complained that latex paint did not flow off the brush as smoothly as oil-based paint.

Recently however, as more states pass laws restricting the use of VOCs, paint manufacturers have put all their research dollars into improving latex paints. Today, many professional painters use oil-based paint only to prime or recoat old oil-based paint.

It is a bad idea to put latex over old oil paint unless you carefully sand or chemically "de-gloss" oil-based surfaces before recoating with latex. On the other hand, it is perfectly fine to use an oil-based primer under latex paint. Some painters do this routinely because oil primer soaks into unpainted surfaces while latex does not.

Choosing Oil-Based Paint. If you do choose to use oil-based paint, mineral

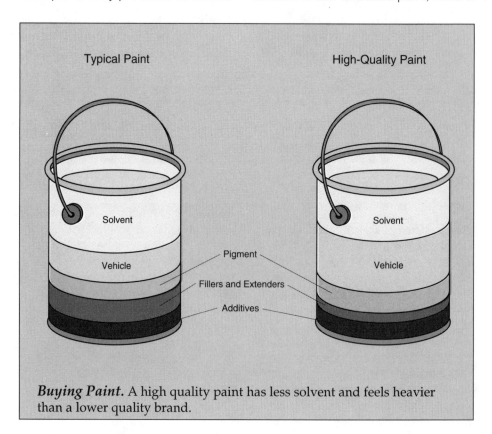

Buying Paint. A high quality paint has less solvent and feels heavier than a lower quality brand.

spirits or turpentine are necessary to clean brushes, rollers, drips and yourself. These solvents are relatively costly (especially compared to water); they smell bad (do not be fooled by labels that say "odorless"); and can be irritating to eyes, nose, lungs and skin. In addition, after you have cleaned tools and skin with mineral spirits, a final cleanup with soap and water is necessary as well.

Usually you have to wait at least overnight before recoating oil-based paint. This can be inconvenient, especially if you can only work on weekends. If the first coat isn't dry on Sunday, you'll wind up waiting a week to finish the job.

Most municipalities have strict rules regarding the disposal of leftover solvents and oil-based paints which means you may find yourself stuck with half-empty containers. In addition, you may end up paying to dispose of excess paint products the same way you would pay to dispose of toxic waste.

Choosing a Sheen

In addition to choosing the color and whether you want latex or oil-based paint, you also need to choose the degree of sheen you want. The range runs from flat to gloss. Most sheens are available in interior or exterior as well as latex or oil-based formulations.

The degree of sheen is determined by the proportion of resin in the paint. The resin determines the degree to which the paint is absorbed into the painted surface and how much pigment is left to form a film on the surface. In short, the more resin, the less the absorption, and thus the glossier the paint.

Flat or Matte. A low-gloss finish hides surface flaws and flaws in prepaint preparation. Because the paint is slightly rough, flat paints do not take scrubbing as well as glossier finishes. Scrubbing flat paint tends to spread out the dirt, leaving a larger dirty spot.

Eggshell and Satin. This is glossier than flat paint, with slightly better abrasion resistance. Satin is glossier than eggshell.

Semi-Gloss. Semi-gloss paints take scrubbing moderately well. They are available in latex or oil-based.

Gloss. This is the highest gloss classification. It is highest in resin and lowest in absorption. Gloss paints take scrubbing well, and are easiest to clean. However, the glossier the paint, the more obvious the surface flaws.

Enamel. Years ago, this term was synonymous with oil-based paint. These days, it is a loose term that refers to the glossiness of paint. The term is reliable only in that you can be reasonably sure that a paint labeled "enamel" is a semi-gloss or gloss paint. One manufacturer's enamel may be glossier than others.

Choosing a Primer

Primer is the paint applied before the topcoat. It is often the difference between high-quality results and poor results. Primers are available in exterior and interior formulations, both oil-based and latex (see page 40).

In general, most experts favor oil-based primer for exterior wood, and latex primer for interior plaster and drywall.

Oil-based primers are used to hide stains on interior surfaces (such as water stains and crayon marks); and to seal stained surfaces, such as kitchen cabinets, which might otherwise "bleed" through a finish coat.

Shellac primers are used as a last resort only if a stain bleeds through oil-based primer. Because they dry in minutes, they are also useful when you cannot wait for primer to dry.

Caution: *Use shellac primers only in very well-ventilated areas. They are alcohol-based and the fumes are very strong.*

Primers for ferrous metals (iron and steel) are different from aluminum primers. The two cannot be used interchangeably.

Choosing a Stain

Stains are essentially pigments dissolved in either an oil- or water-based vehicle. When you want to enhance the natural wood grain stain is the finish of choice.

Interior Stains. These stains come in many wood-tone colors. They are most typically used on interior woodwork and furniture. Interior stains are typically covered with a clear topcoat such as varnish.

Exterior Stains. These stains are essentially paints with reduced amounts of pigment and are used on solid wood and plywood siding. There are two types of exterior stains. Semi-transparent stain adds color but reveals the grain. Solid stains obscure the grain but are thinner than paint. Because stains are thinner than paint, they soak into the wood. As a result, stain does not peel or crack the way paint does, and you can add new coats through the years without worrying about building up layers that eventually have to be stripped off. Another advantage is that stains do not require primer.

There is a downside to the reduced amounts of pigment in stains. Pigment plays a big part in resisting the weather and sunlight that break paint down. Houses that have been painted with semi-transparent stains must be recoated more frequently than houses coated with solid stains. All stained houses must be recoated more frequently than painted houses. The more severe the weather conditions (heat, humidity, direct sun) in your part of the country, the less suitable exterior stain becomes for your home.

Choosing Tools

It is rare to come across a paint job that cannot be done quickest and best with brushes and rollers, the meat and potatoes of painting tools. Brushes work well because they have narrow sides for narrow edges, broad sides for broad surfaces, and bristles that can be tweaked to fit into tight spots. When used on large flat areas, roller nap mimics brush bristles. Brush and roller technique comes naturally. People know almost instinctively which way to turn a brush, or when a brush needs to be reloaded. It is easy to feel when a roller is skipping or pulling. If you buy the right brushes and rollers and use them properly, they are all you need to apply the paint.

However, there are other gadgets on the market such as foam painting pads, foam brushes (pads on a stick), power rollers and sprayers.

Getting the Basic Brush

Always use the highest-quality brush you can afford. Just as with the paint, buy at or very near the top of the line. Cheap brushes are never good brushes. Among the costlier brushes, some are better than others.

If you are going to buy only one brush, you can do most any job with a 3-inch flat brush with a tapered bottom. This brush lets you brush out large surfaces easily while it's tapered bottom helps paint a crisp line.

Choosing Other Brushes

The following brushes are useful for specific jobs.

Flat Brush. A four-inch or three-inch wide brush, with a tapered edge, is the most common and most useful type of brush. It can cover large areas and make hard cut lines.

Sash Brush. This brush has angled bristles that are ideal for making crisp lines on trim, molding and window muntins.

Stain Brush. The bristle area on this brush is shorter and wider than a paint brush to counteract the tendency stain has to drip into the brush ferrule.

Foam Brush. This tool consists of a foam pad on a stick. Its primary usefulness is that it is cheap and disposable. Some good foam brush jobs include applying stain, and painting window muntins (the tapered edge is the perfect size). Do not use foam brushes for applying paint remover because they melt.

Rough-Surface Painter. This is a combination brush and paint pad, useful for painting rough surfaces such as exterior wood shingles. It looks like a scrub brush.

Selecting the Right Bristles

Whatever type of brush you choose, you'll have two kinds of bristles to choose from:

Nylon Bristles. These are best used for latex paint although they also can be used for oil-based paint.

Natural Bristle. Also called "China bristle," natural bristle brushes are preferred for use with oil-based paints and varnishes. They cost 40 to 50 percent more than synthetic-bristle brushes.

Note: Do not use natural bristle brushes for latex paint. The water in the paint ruins the brush.

Getting the Basic Brush. When buying a brush check for thick, soft, resilient bristles held in place by a sturdy ferrule.

3" Flat Brush — Handle — Ferrule — Heel — Bristles

3" Flat Brush · Sash Brush · Stain Brush · 4" Flat Brush · Foam Brush · Rough Surface Painter

Choosing Other Brushes. Certain painting jobs require brushes designed for specific tasks. Above are the most common types of brushes. These brushes can be found at home centers, paint stores and hardware stores.

■ Tug gently on the bristles. If more than a few pull out, do not buy the brush.

■ Bounce and wiggle the bristles in your palm. A good brush has bristles that feel soft and springy, and bounce back into shape quickly when you let go.

■ Make sure bristles are thick and plentiful. Fold back the bristles with your hand, and look at the place they connect to the handle. If you see a lot of handle between a few plugs of bristles, you have an inferior brush. Good brushes have bristles that are at least 2 inches long. A good brush that is 1 or 2 inches wide has bristles that are about 3 inches long. A good brush that is 3 or 4 inches wide has bristles about 4 inches long.

■ Check the metal ferrule that holds the bristles to the handle. It must be substantial (not thin and flimsy) and firmly attached to the handle. Make sure it does not rock when the bristles are wiggled back and forth.

Choosing Rollers

The two parts to a paint roller include the handle (also called the frame) and the cover. As with brushes, the first rule of choosing a roller is: Do not buy cheap. Poor quality roller handles bend with pressure. Choose a good quality handle that feels comfortable in your hand and has some substance. Use the highest-quality covers. The price difference between the cheapest and most expensive nylon cover is only a few dollars.

Roll the cover in your hand. The nap of a good roller has an even consistency, with no bumps or flat spots. Tug gently on the nap; if any fuzz comes off, find a better cover.

Nylon Roller Covers. These covers are suitable for most paint jobs. They are available in short, medium and long nap. Medium nap is a good choice for walls and ceilings; long nap is suitable for painting concrete, brick, or other rough surfaces. Short nap can provide a smooth finish for very flat surfaces. Short nap covers hold relatively little paint so more effort goes into frequent reloading of the roller and keeping a wet edge. Nylon covers can be stored wet from day-to-day during a paint job. You can preserve a nylon roller for the next job by cleaning it out thoroughly. You may decide, however, that cleaning the roller is not worth the few dollars saved.

Lamb's Wool Covers. These are expensive, high-quality rollers. If you thoroughly clean and carefully dry a lamb's wool cover, it can be used for many paint jobs. These covers produce a distinctive, slightly stippled effect. Some people like the finish; others hate it. Test the finish in an inconspicuous area such as a closet. If you like it, use the cover for the whole paint job.

Doughnut Rollers. These small, one-piece foam rollers are good for moldings and corners. Some painters find them indispensable, while others do every job with only brushes and a standard 9-inch roller. Small foam rollers are inexpensive, so try one.

Foam Rollers. These are useful for painting cabinets and vanities because they speed up the job and do not leave a stipple like the rollers mentioned above.

Choosing a Roller Pan

For interior work, pick a deep, sturdy metal roller pan. Stay away from flimsy metal and plastic pans. (Most shrink-wrapped kits, consisting of a poor-quality brush and roller stuck in a cheap pan, do not provide good results.) Pick up the pan and twist it. If it pops in and out of shape, do not buy it. In general, a deeper pan is best, it allows you to get more work done between refills.

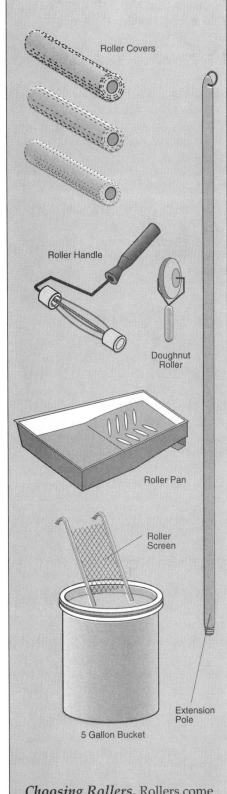

Roller Covers

Roller Handle

Doughnut Roller

Roller Pan

Roller Screen

Extension Pole

5 Gallon Bucket

Choosing Rollers. Rollers come in different materials with varying depth of nap. Use one that best covers the texture of the surface being painted. You want a roller handle that does not bend, and a roller pan that is deep and sturdy.

For exterior jobs, metal roller screens that fit into 5-gallon buckets are preferable to pans.

Paint stores sell handy 2 1/2-gallon square buckets that take a roller screen and have a lip for pouring paint back into a can. Because of their shape they do not move or spin when hanging off a hook on the side of a ladder.

Choosing a Paint Pad

Foam pads do not reach into tight spots, they are slower than rollers, and their shape does not allow for basic maneuvers such as feathering edges.

Using Sprayers

Paint sprayers are specialty tools that you may find too expensive or too difficult to use. They are, however, great time-savers. Professional painters use sprayers for fast coverage of large areas, and for hard-to-brush items such as shutters, gates and trellises.

Types of Sprayers

There are two basic types of sprayers: propulsion and compressed air. Both provide similar results.

Propulsion Sprayer. This type of machine is an electrically driven sprayer that "flips" or "spits" out small droplets of paint. In inexpensive models, the unit is fed by a small pot of paint. These sprayers are excellent for small areas that are difficult to paint with a brush, such as louvered shutters or wicker furniture. More expensive models, generally used by professionals, have a hose that is connected to a larger pail of paint, and an adjustable rate of spray mist and pressure. These machines are excellent for spraying siding.

Compressed Air Sprayer. This type of sprayer is also electric. It emits a finer mist of paint that is driven by forced air shot through the paint. These units cover large surfaces

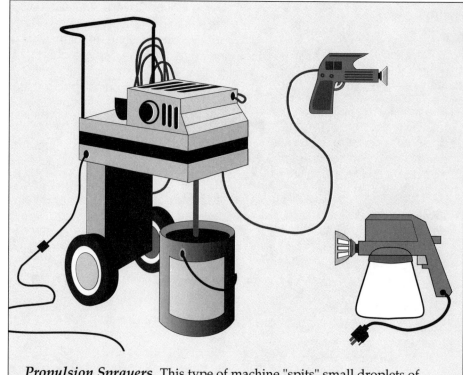

Propulsion Sprayers. This type of machine "spits" small droplets of paint. The larger machines are used by professional painters.

with a smooth finish, but they are too expensive to justify for a single paint job. However, with the proper attachments, the air compressor can be used for nail guns and auto repair.

Spray Cans. Spray paint is great for a quick paint job on a metal stair railing, or some other fairly small item, such as a mailbox. The cost per square foot is high, so you do not want to paint a large item with spray cans. Always buy one can more than you think you need. Spray cans always seem to run out 90 percent of the way through the job.

Compressed Air Sprayer. This machine shoots air through the paint reservoir creating a fine paint mist.

Using Power Rollers

Power rollers, simply explained, are devices that pump paint from a can or reservoir through a specially made roller body. (Most include paint pads as an accessory.) The idea, which is a good one, is to eliminate the 50 percent of rolling time that a painter spends getting paint out of the pan or bucket. The execution, which is not so good, comprises the questionable marriage of painting and plumbing.

There are three types of power rollers commonly available. One employs a small dolly, which holds a paint can and a pump. The dolly rides along behind you as you paint. The problem: Pulled along by the paint hose, the dolly is not likely to ride so well across drop cloths.

Another power roller has the paint in a reservoir, which you sling over your shoulder. This is a better idea than the dolly, but you have to "undress" every time you want to top off the reservoir.

A third power roller sucks paint out of the can and into a long roller handle. You push the handle, like a syringe, to force paint into the roller. The problems: You still have to stop to refill, and it is difficult to control the roller as you try to paint and simultaneously push the syringe.

Power rollers are for latex paint only. When you finish, hook up the pump to your kitchen sink or an outside hose faucet, and run water through the whole apparatus.

Pole Sander. If you are going to paint a room that has new drywall, or a room that has been substantially patched, you will need a pole sander to smooth drywall joints or plaster patches. The sander "extends" your

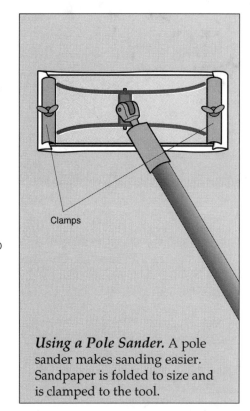

Clamps

Using a Pole Sander. A pole sander makes sanding easier. Sandpaper is folded to size and is clamped to the tool.

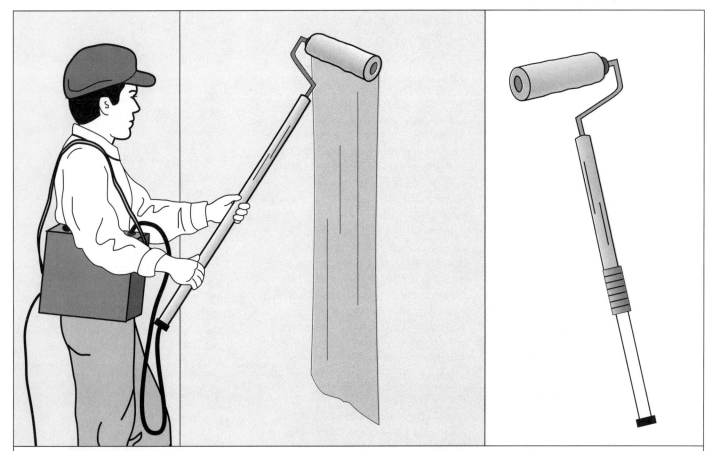

Using Power Rollers. The different types of power rollers vary in how paint is supplied to the roller head. Shown at left is a roller with a paint reservoir slung over the user's shoulder. At right is a roller that stores paint in the long handle.

If you find you must thin paint, read the manufacturer's directions which are printed on the can and follow these guidelines:

■ Mix well as you add the thinner slowly and carefully. You can always add more thinner, but you cannot remove it.

■ If possible thin a batch of paint big enough to do the whole job. If that isn't practical, thin a quantity of paint that allows you to paint to a logical break (for instance, one wall of a house). This way, slight variations in color and gloss are not as apparent. Reserve some thinned paint to use for touch-ups.

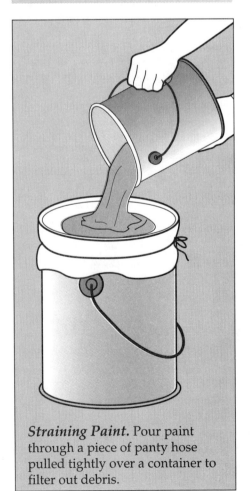

Straining Paint. Pour paint through a piece of panty hose pulled tightly over a container to filter out debris.

arms so you can cover a large area while standing in one spot. It also extends your sanding stroke, making the sanded joints consistent.

Extension Handles. For painting ceilings or exterior siding such as Texture 1-11, (T-1-11) you need an extension handle for your roller. Many painters like to use an extension to minimize bending when rolling walls: You can keep the roller tray on the floor and step toward the wall to move the roller up. Unlike other equipment, you need not necessarily buy the best one you can afford. Virtually any extension handle, down to the simplest broom-handle type works fine. If you need an extension handle that changes sizes, such as a 4-, 8- and 12-foot aluminum handle, check the couplings for smooth operation, and buy one that feels sturdy when extended.

Thinning, Mixing & Straining

Thinning Paint

As a general rule, you do not need to thin paint for a house-painting job. When you get the paint home from the store, it is already mixed properly. However, if you accumulate and store an inventory of paint, some of the paint vehicle is likely to evaporate and you will have to thin it before it can be used. Another circumstance in which you may have to thin paint is when you are working in hot, dry weather. The thinner helps to make the paint flow properly. A simpler solution, however, is to plan your projects f or spring or fall when the weather is mild.

The type of thinner used varies according to the type of paint used. Latex paints are thinned with water; oil-based paints are thinned with mineral spirits turpentine or brand-name thinners. Read the instructions on the paint can for specifics.

Mixing Paint

Have the paint dealer shake the paint before you take it home. Then mix the paint with a stir stick just before you begin work, to ensure even color. To avoid spills, mix the paint in a bucket (not in the can) but be sure to get all the sediment out of the can because that is where the pigment settles. If you know you need five gallons or more, buy the paint premixed in five-gallon buckets.

Straining Paint

There are two good reasons for straining paint: to get rid of the grit and to remove paint that has hardened.

Sometimes during a paint job (typically an exterior job), the brush picks up grit from the work surface and deposits it in the paint bucket. If this happens, the grit finds its way back onto your brush, causing streaks and skips as you apply the paint. If your brush gets gritty, pour the paint through a piece of panty hose and clean the brush.

Stored paint, or paint left in a container that was not properly sealed, tends to skim over. This paint must be strained. Pour the paint through a piece of panty hose. If the skin flops out, pull it out of the way and discard it.

Getting the Job Done Safely

As with all do-it-yourself projects there are cautions to observe and precautions to take. Always use safety equipment to protect your eyes and lungs, practice ladder safety, and be aware of the chemical hazards posed by fumes and lead in old paint.

Using Ladders

Most people find they can work comfortably on six- to eight-foot ladders. However when working on ladders taller than that, natural

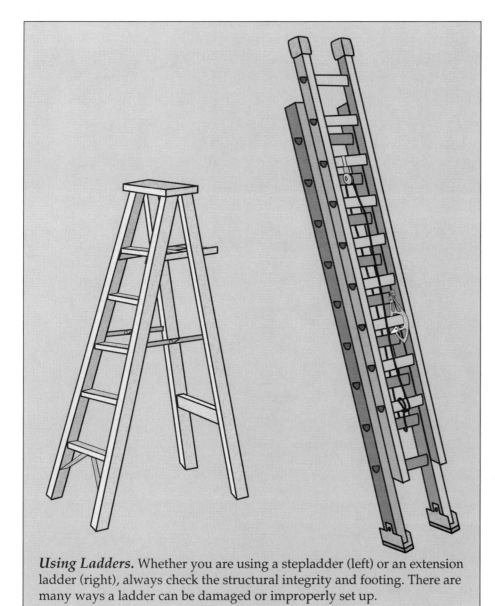

Using Ladders. Whether you are using a stepladder (left) or an extension ladder (right), always check the structural integrity and footing. There are many ways a ladder can be damaged or improperly set up.

balance, confidence and experience come into play. Consider the disadvantages before you commit to working with tall extension ladders. Buying the ladders, scaffolding, ladder jacks, and other equipment needed to paint an average two-story house quickly consumes the savings of a do-it-yourself job. (And you will not need the equipment again for several years.) If the ladder is rented or borrowed, inspect it carefully for signs of damage or abuse. Do not use the ladder if the hooks do not lock cleanly, the ladder feet are damaged, the rungs or side rails are cracked, the joints are loose, or if it is twisted.

If you plan to buy a ladder, remember that the last thing you want is a cheap, flimsy ladder. Buy the best ladder you can afford, even if it is only a five-foot ladder. Aluminum ladders are lightest and wood ones are the heaviest. Fiberglass ladders are electrically non-conductive. Good fiberglass ladders are sturdy and tolerant of a wide range of conditions (heat, cold, wet, dry). They have a long service life but are fairly heavy.

Finding Lead in Paint

If you are working in an area with peeling and flaking paint, consult an environmental engineer for advice on how best to deal with it. Some states and municipalities have laws that

require lead abatement before a new occupant moves into a house. Consult with local environment agencies so that you are aware of the requirements in your area.

Any house paint applied before the mid 1970s is likely to contain lead. Even paints applied into the mid 1980s may contain some lead. (Lead was a common pigment until 1969; it was an additive until 1978. Some of this paint stayed in retailers' or painters' inventories for years.) Prep work that involves sanding or scraping paint that was applied before the mid 80s is likely to create lead-laced chips and dust.

Kits that detect lead are available in many hardware stores and home center stores. Test for lead, and for best safety, always assume paint applied before the mid 1980s contains lead.

The inhalation or ingestion of lead causes lead poisoning. Symptoms include, but are not limited to, aches and pains, fatigue, confusion, and in extreme cases, irreversible brain damage. Children and fetuses are particularly susceptible.

When doing preparation work that may disturb lead paint, follow these common-sense precautions:

■ Keep children, pregnant women, and women who may be pregnant away from the work site until dust and chips are cleaned up. Sweep up chips, vacuum dust and damp-mop the floors.

■ Drape and tape work areas. Hang polyethylene sheeting on door and window openings, and secure the sheeting with duct tape.

■ Clean up all dust and chips at the end of every work day. Wash work clothes every day. Change clothes and shower before taking lunch or dinner breaks.

■ Have your pediatrician check your child's lead level. This fairly simple and inexpensive test is a good idea whether you are working with lead paint or not.

Providing Ventilation. Proper ventilation assists the removal of irritating fumes.

Providing Ventilation

Even latex paint fumes can be irritating to eyes, nose, lungs and skin. When painting inside, open enough windows to provide good cross-ventilation. For best ventilation, put a fan in a window and set it up so that it blows air out of the room. Wear a respirator if you are using a compressed-air spraying system. If you have heart or respiratory problems, consult a doctor before starting a prep or paint job. Wearing a respirator causes labored breathing, and puts people with heart or respiratory problems at risk.

Changing Filters. Prep work and sanding creates dust. Check heat- and air filters frequently during the job, and change them when they get dirty. Always change filters after prep work and after final cleanup.

Wearing Eye Protection

Wear goggles during sanding or scraping, or any other prep work that sends debris flying. In addition, paint flecks that fall into your eyes hurt, and cleaning oil paint out of lashes can be very unpleasant, so it is a good idea to wear safety glasses while painting (especially when using oil-based paint).

Using a Respirator

For paint removal and related work, you may need more than a nuisance-rated dust mask (a paper mask with one rubber band). When sanding, wear a respirator that's NIOSH-rated for dust and fibers. Drywall and plaster dust causes permanent damage to bronchi and lungs. The best disposable dust masks have an exhalation valve which increases comfort. If there is a chance of

encountering asbestos (commonly used in buildings until the late 1970s), wear a half-mask respirator rated for asbestos. When working with coatings that produce fumes that may be toxic (for instance, some lacquers and paint removers), wear a respirator that is NIOSH-rated for toxic fumes. The best respirators are reusable half-mask respirators, which require a set of prefilters in addition to the regular filters.

Changing Filters. Change filters after any dust producing job.

EXTERIOR PAINTING

You can save a lot of money by painting the outside of your house yourself. In this chapter you will learn about the tools and techniques needed to ensure safety, cost effectiveness and professional-looking results.

Time to Paint?

Is it obvious when a house needs painting? The answer to that question is "usually". If you would like new colors on the house, or if the existing paint is clearly in bad shape, then the house needs painting.

Start with a visual inspection of the house. If yours is a two-story with complicated angles, you may have to look out second-floor windows or use binoculars to see everything. Check the existing paint for problems such as blistering, peeling, alligatoring and cracking (all discussed in this chapter). If a significant amount of paint is coming off the house, there is a paint job in your future.

Washing the House

Sometimes a house is dirty and needs a bath. If you are happy with the color of the house and the paint is in good shape, you can simply wash the house (or have a house-washing contractor do it for you).

Painting Siding

While aluminum and vinyl siding are perfectly good materials when applied to new construction, they are not maintenance-free coverings, and neither cures the problems that result in frequent repainting. In fact, installing siding over peeling paint without curing the problems that caused the peeling in the first place, creates more of a problem and may cause extensive rot.

Siding fades, gets dirty, and is susceptible to mold and mildew stains, just like any other house cladding. While siding typically carries a long-term guarantee against such things as cracking, splitting and denting, siding looks just as bad as any surface after ten years of rain, wind, and or snow. Think of it this way: What would an expensive car look like if you parked it in the middle of your yard and did not move it for ten years? At the very least, siding requires a good washing from time to time.

Consider the expenses before choosing these sidings for your house. While it is often promoted as a money-saver, the truth is that usually a house can be prepped and painted many times over for less than the cost of siding. In general, paint works best and costs less.

Some contractors wash a small inconspicuous area of the house as a sample of their work. Washing the house is done at a fraction of the cost of a top-to-bottom paint job.

Selecting the Proper Paint

There are several reasons latex paints are preferred over oil-based paints for exterior work. First, there is performance. Latex paints dry to a rubbery film, which takes the flexing that results from changes in temperature and humidity. Simply put, latex paint stays on the house better than oil-based paint.

Second, by using latex paint, you avoid the entire problem concerning volatile organic compounds (VOCs), which are the gaseous forms of the solvents that evaporate from oil-based paint. Some VOCs are known health and environmental threats; while others are strong suspects. Some states and municipalities have made it virtually impossible to obtain and apply oil-based paint.

The third reason is cost. Latex paint costs less than oil-based paint. And with latex, you do not have to buy expensive solvents for clean up—soap and water is sufficient.

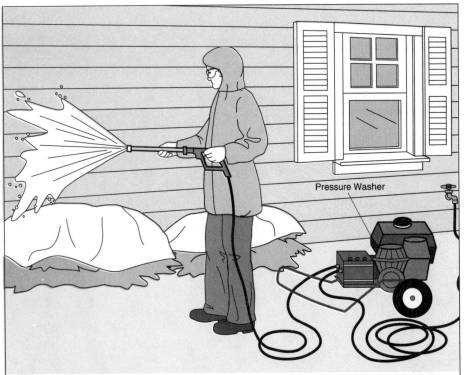

Washing the House. Before you paint, consider having a house-washing contractor clean the outside of the house. You might discover the house doesn't need painting at all.

Pressure Washer

Painting in Hot Weather. If paint dries too quickly it will not adhere properly. In warmer weather (over 70°F) avoid painting in direct sunlight.

Painting in Cold Weather. When working in cool weather (55-70°F) follow the sun's motion to obtain quicker drying.

Watching the Weather

The only drawback to using latex outside is you have to be much more aware of the weather than with oil-based paints. Latex is much less tolerant of temperature extremes than oil-based paint. And because water is the solvent for latex, rain can wash the paint away if it hasn't had a chance to dry.

Painting in Hot Weather

The hotter the weather, the quicker latex paint dries. When paint dries too fast it causes the following problems: brushes and rollers gum up; paint fails to bond properly with the surface underneath it; and uneven drying causes uneven gloss.

The ideal painting temperature is around 70 degrees Fahrenheit, although you can do a perfectly good job when the temperature is in the 90s. If the temperature is between 55 and 70 degrees, plan your work so that you are in the sun. If the weather is warmer, stay out of direct sunlight. During hot weather,

do not paint on windy days because wind speeds up drying even more.

Painting in Cold Weather

Latex paint does not cure at temperatures below about 45 degrees Fahrenheit. That is why manufacturers' specifications always call for latex paint to be applied at temperatures no lower than 50 degrees. It is best to plan paint jobs for spring, summer or early fall. Do not paint when the mercury falls below 50 degrees. There are few things more discouraging than watching paint slide off the walls in sheets.

Checking for Moisture

It is okay to apply latex paint to a surface that is slightly damp (cool to the touch) but not wet. Let wet surfaces dry out before painting. If rain or dew gets on latex paint before it is dry, symptoms range from nothing, to mottling, to blistering, to washing off entirely. If the paint bubbles it has to be scraped or sanded off and the surface repainted.

Tying Back Trees & Shrubbery

Before painting, figure out the "footprints" of your ladders or scaffolding, and where your equipment and body will be as you work your way around the house. Plants that rub against the surfaces you will be painting, and branches that interfere with your access to the house, have to be pruned or tied back. If a little judicious pruning allows you good access, break out the gardening tools and consider the pruning part of your prep work. Of course, there are right ways and wrong ways to prune trees, and bad pruning can severely damage plants. If you are not up to speed on pruning, most home and garden centers sell books and pamphlets on the subject. If in doubt, hire a landscape contractor to do the work.

Branches that cannot be pruned can be tied back temporarily. Cover shrubs with old bed sheets, tie them up with ropes, pull them away from the house, and tie the ropes to stakes

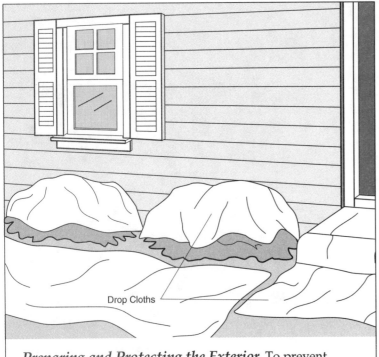

Preparing and Protecting the Exterior. To prevent damage and to allow clear access to siding, tie back trees and shrubs and use drop cloths to catch drips and spills.

Using Ladders and Scaffolding. If you need scaffolding, rather than just a ladder for your paint job, consider having it done professionally.

in the ground. Do not use plastic to cover plants; the plastic acts as a greenhouse, and cooks the plants. Heavy drop cloths may bend or break plants.

Caution: *Do not climb into a tree with a saw. Working on tall trees is a job for professionals.*

Using Drop Cloths

Even the most careful painter creates splats and drips. Drop cloths protect surfaces from these mishaps. The correct use of drop cloths is one of the many things that can make the difference between a professional-quality job and a major mess. Canvas drop cloths are best; they hold up to heavy use, absorbing paint drips and most spills. Thinner fabric drop cloths are reasonably good, although big drips or spills soak through them. Thin plastic drop cloths are not good for use underfoot, but they are useful for covering surfaces such as iron railings or prefinished gutters.

Use drop cloths to cover steps, walkways, porch floors, decks,

patios, and any other surfaces you want to protect. It is best to cover the surfaces along one whole side of the house. Continual moving of cloths tends to leave a trail of drips and paint chips. Be careful when walking over drop cloths; they are notorious for developing wrinkles that catch your feet and ladder.

Never put a ladder on a drop cloth over slick surfaces such as slate. The ladder can slip. For best stability, place ladder feet on the soil, not on hard landscape surfaces.

Using Ladders & Scaffolding

If yours is a modern one-story house built on a slab or low foundation, you can probably reach most of the house with an 8-foot stepladder.

Taller houses, or houses with tall eaves, require the use of an extension ladder. A modern two-story house requires at least one 28-foot extension ladder. (Older houses, which have taller stories, require

taller ladders.) Working on a tall extension ladder is not for every-body. Good extension ladders are expensive and heavy, and require a large amount of storage space.

If the job requires working on a tall extension ladder, carefully consider whether you want to take it on. The savings gained by painting the house is quickly wiped out by a visit to the hospital.

Most homeowners do not own scaffolding (sometimes called staging). If your job requires scaffolding, the most likely sources are rental stores or a contractor who assembles the scaffolding and disassembles it when the job is done. Typically, scaffolding is rented by the week or the month. If your job requires scaffolding, it might be less expensive to hire a painting contractor to do the whole job. If you plan to paint only on weekends, the result will be a hefty rental fee. A full-time painting crew is able to get the job done a lot faster than you can.

Using Stepladders

Stepladders are available in a range of heights, from short, 36-inch step stools to tall ladders used for specialized jobs such as tree trimming.

Most people are comfortable on an 8-foot stepladder. Ladder height is figured by the length of the ladder's side rails. The side rails are not vertical when the ladder is deployed, so a 8-foot ladder is not quite 8-foot high.

Stepladders are available in aluminum, fiberglass, and wood. Of the three, aluminum ladders are lightest, fiberglass ladders are somewhat heavier, and wood ladders are heaviest of all. Aluminum and fiberglass ladders are the best choice, as wood ladders tend to deteriorate when exposed to weather. Fiberglass ladders have the added advantage of non-conductive side rails which offer some protection if a ladder accidentally touches a live wire. Of course, extreme caution must be used around live wires. A fiberglass ladder is not a guarantee against shocks.

As with other equipment, always buy the best ladder you can afford. Some inexpensive aluminum ladders bend under the weight of a heavy person. If you weigh more than 200 pounds, buy at least a middle-grade ladder.

Taking Precautions. Stepladders are labeled with warnings. Heed them when they tell you not to step

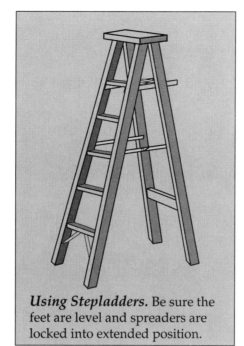

Using Stepladders. Be sure the feet are level and spreaders are locked into extended position.

on the top step or top of the ladder. It is very easy to lose your balance.

If you are working with two stepladders of differing heights, use the taller ladder first, and then switch to the shorter one. If you work on a ladder for awhile, your body tends to "remember" the number of steps on the ladder. If you switch from, say, a 5-foot ladder to an 8-foot ladder, you will have a tendency to step off the taller ladder before you reach the bottom rung.

Make sure that the four ladder feet are level and stable. Place stable blocks under ladder feet that do not reach the ground. Dig out under feet that are "too long." Make sure the ladder is opened completely, and

that the spreaders are locked. If the ladder rails bow, or if the ladder twists, get off the ladder and make sure it is square and stable. If bowing or twisting persists, the ladder may be defective.

Using Extension Ladders

The standard-issue extension ladder is a trusty 16-footer. This type of ladder takes you to the roof of most one-story houses. Extension ladders are available at dizzying heights, but most people are uncomfortable on

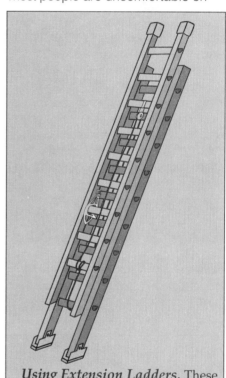

Using Extension Ladders. These ladders consist of two sections. One section rides inside the other and is raised by a rope and pulley.

Ladder Ratings

Ladders typically are rated in the following way:

- Class 1—200 pound capacity
- Class 2—225 pound capacity
- Class 3—300 pound capacity

(Ratings are labeled on the ladder.)

Federal regulations require that ladders be tested to a safety factor of three. That is, a Class 1 ladder

is designed to hold a static weight (standing still) of 600 pounds. This seems like a big built-in safety factor, and it is. However, for most people it is the bouncing of the ladder that makes climbing uncomfortable, and a Class 1 ladder will bounce when a 200-pound person climbs it.

The higher the rating of the ladder, the heavier the ladder. A typical 28-foot Class 1 aluminum ladder

weighs about 40 pounds; a Class 2 weighs about 45 pounds; and a Class 3 weighs about 60 pounds.

Buy the heaviest-duty ladder you can afford and handle. Remember that a ladder is a lever, and because of this, it may be able to move you easier than you can move it. This becomes obvious when you try to carry and deploy a 60-pound, 24-foot-long ladder.

anything taller than a 24- to 28-foot ladder. Also, moving a ladder much bigger than this is a two-person job.

The highest point on a house is the peak on the gable ends. You can estimate how much ladder you need by figuring about 12 feet for each story of the house, then adding the height of the foundation, and the height of the roof peak. Your working height will be about three or four feet less than the length of the ladder. For instance, a 28-foot ladder actually brings you about 24 feet off the ground.

Checking for Level. Make sure the ladder feet are level before climbing. You can use bricks, sound pieces of two-by lumber, or specially-made leveling attachments to level the ladder feet. Make sure the blocks are securely planted on the ground. Do not climb on windy days. Wind can move a ladder, and a person standing on a ladder.

During prep work or priming, you can move a relatively short ladder sideways by climbing down, moving the bottom, then sliding the top of the ladder along the house. If windows are in the way, "jump" the ladder over them by pulling the top out slightly away from the house.

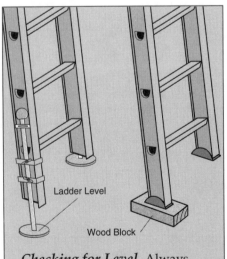

Checking for Level. Always check that the feet are level before climbing a ladder. You can use blocks or special leveling devices. Never place a ladder on a slick or wet surface.

Ladder Level

Wood Block

1 Protect siding by wrapping the top ends of extension ladders with foam or rags.

If the ladder is particularly tall or heavy; or, if you are working on the finish coat, do not slide the ladder across the house. Take the ladder down as described on page 27, carry it to the new location and reset it.

Do not leave ladders standing unattended. Children may decide to climb them, and wind blows them down.

Raising Extension Ladders

The best way to carry an extension ladder is to grab it at the center, hold it at pants-pocket height, and carry it like a briefcase. If the ladder is longer than 16 feet, you might need a helper to carry the ladder. Raising an extension ladder may take some practice.

1 **Protecting the Siding.** Before deploying the ladder, wrap the upper ends with old socks, or tape on some foam, to prevent scarring the siding.

2 **Raising the Ladder.** Place the feet of the ladder firmly on the ground, then walk toward the house, allowing your hands to "climb" down the rungs.

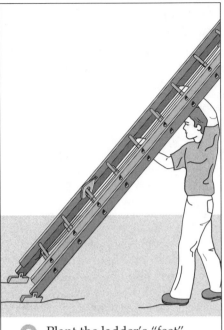

2 Plant the ladder's "feet" securely before raising it.

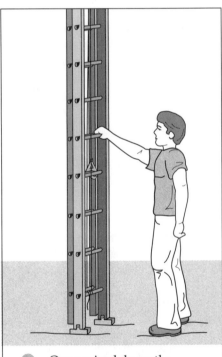

3 Once raised, keep the ladder vertical. Ladders are top-heavy and easily fall over.

3 **Keeping the Ladder Vertical.** Once the ladder is raised, take care to keep it vertical. If the top wanders significantly to one side, you might not be able to keep it from crashing down.

Lowering Extension Ladders

Have someone help you when lowering a long extension ladder.

1 Dropping the Ladder. With a helper "footing" the ladder to stabilize it, drop the ladder sideways. Keep one hand on the ladder.

2 Positioning for the Catch. As the helper balances the ladder, move out to catch it at the midpoint.

1 Have a helper brace the ladder foot.

2 Helper slowly lowers the ladder as you move toward top end.

The ideal ladder angle is about 70 degrees. At this angle, the feet of a 28-foot ladder hits the ground about 72 inches from the wall. (The ratio is about one foot away from the wall for every four feet of actual ladder height.) Before starting the job, make sure the area where the feet land is readily accessible all the way around the house.

3 Catching the Ladder. Using your free hand, catch a rung near the top of the ladder.

4 Carrying the Ladder. Use both arms to stabilize the ladder and then carry it at waist height.

3 Stabilize the falling ladder by moving quickly toward the top.

4 Carry the ladder horizontally at waist level. Two people may be necessary.

Hazards Up High

Electricity. Do not work near live electrical wires. If there is any way you or your ladder can touch the wires, call the utility company and have them disconnect the incoming service wires (the wires from the utility pole to the house).

Bees and Wasps. Bees build hives in exterior walls. Bees are usually fairly obvious—you can see them coming and going through a hole in the house. Don't try to fight bees. Call an exterminator.

A careful prepainting inspection of the house may reveal wasp nests under the eaves. Irradicate nests with long-range wasp and hornet spray. This is one of those cases where using poison is preferable to running into wasps at the top of an extension ladder.

The most dangerous wasps are those hidden behind soffit or fascia boards. Wasps find tiny holes in the trim, then build nests in the attic. Use an extension pole to tap along the area where you are working. If wasps appear, call an exterminator.

Using Ladder Jacks

Ladder jacks are brackets that support a scaffolding plank between two ladders. Using ladder jacks provides a small, simple scaffold that two people can set up. Painting while standing on the scaffolding requires concentration. You cannot forget that you are standing on a 12-inch-wide platform. Inexperienced people have been known to get comfortable moving from side to side, so much so they forget where they are, and take an unfortunate step back.

Ladder jacks are useful when you are working in one area for an extended period, or when working on an area that you cannot get a single ladder exactly where you need it (such as dead center on an upstairs window).

A ladder jack scaffold comprises two ladders, a set of ladder jacks (which resemble shelf brackets), and a scaffold plank. Always use a proper plank, which is typically aluminum. Planks and ladder jacks are available at home center stores and rental stores. Resist any urges to press scrap lumber into service as a scaffolding plank. Always have a helper to

Using Ladder Jacks. Ladder jacks provide simple, portable scaffolding for one or two people.

install the plank. Each person climbs a ladder, holding an end of the plank. Once the plank is in place, you do not need the helper again until it is time to take the scaffolding down.

1 Setting up the Ladder Jacks. Carry up each ladder jack and secure it properly at equal heights on both ladders.

2 Bringing Up One End. Bring one end of the plank up one of

1 Carry the jacks up the ladder and secure them to the rungs.

Ladder Jack

Plank

2 Bring one end of the plank up one ladder and put it over the jack.

Calculating Paint Coverage

Paint coverage is affected by many factors, such as surface absorption, masonry texture, and environmental factors. Old bare wood sucks up paint; and textured surfaces have many more square feet of surface than can be calculated merely by multiplying width times height. If calculations result in, for instance, 10.3 gallons of paint, it is best to buy 11 gallons. Having too little paint means another trip to the store, and the risk of not being able to properly match colors. Besides, it is a good idea to have some extra paint for future touch-ups.

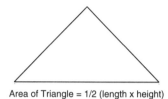

Area of Triangle = 1/2 (length x height)

Area of Rectangle = length x height

Coverage Rates

The following calculations assume one coat of latex paint or primer, with a typical coverage rate of about 400 square feet per gallon.

- Smooth wood siding, unpainted: 250 square feet per gallon (about 200 for narrow lap siding)

- Smooth wood siding, painted: 350 square feet per gallon (about 280 for narrow lap siding)

- Stucco wall, unpainted: 150 square feet per gallon

- Stucco wall, painted: 250 square feet per gallon

- Shingles, unpainted: 200 square feet per gallon

- Shingles, painted: 250 square feet per gallon

- Doors: 12 doors per gallon

the ladders while a helper remains on the ground supporting the other end of the plank.

3 Bringing Up the Other End. Rest one end of the plank on a jack. Hold it in place while the helper brings up the other end.

4 Securing the Plank. Flip the plank into position. Make sure it is securely held by the jacks and extends at least 12 inches over each end.

3 While stabilizing the raised end, carry the other end of the plank up. The first end juts over the jack as the second end comes up.

4 Place plank on jacks. Check for adequate overhang on both sides.

One Coat or Two?

Some paints, typically higher-quality paints, are marketed as one-coat paints. Surely, the idea of one-coat painting has its attractions. One coat requires half as much material and half as much time. However, you cannot always count on paint to provide good results with just one coat. First of all, you do not want one thick coat of paint. A coating that is too thick does not cure and adhere properly. Secondly, if you are painting over a dark color with a light color, it is almost guaranteed that you will need two coats of paint to properly and entirely cover the darker color.

For a first-time paint job on raw wood or siding, apply a primer coat, and two top coats. However, if you are repainting a house in a color similar to the existing color, after prep and priming, one coat may provide perfectly acceptable results.

With older houses, consider limiting the paint job to one coat, even though it might not last as long as a two-coat job. The more coats of paint on the house, the more likely the paint is to peel. Eventually, built-up paint reaches a "critical mass," and starts to come off in chunks. Moving parts such as doors and windows bind as paint builds up. Sometimes, one more coat of paint can be the difference between an operational door and a door that sticks shut. Finally, too much paint obscures detail. Fancy moldings on older houses often loose detail because of thick layers of paint.

Staining as an Alternative

Stain is a good alternative to paint for houses that are clad with solid wood such as redwood, cedar or cypress. It allows the wood grain to show, and provides a handsome natural finish.

Stains are available in latex and oil-based formulations. Both work well. Stains are essentially thinned paint; and are available in varying opacities, from clear to nearly opaque. Stains penetrate wood more than paint, but because paint forms an outer layer of skin on wood, it provides better protection from the weather.

A stained house requires more maintenance than a painted house. The coating has to be renewed more often. Old stain does not peel like old paint. Instead, it wears away, leaving the wood exposed to the weather.

Heat and humidity are tough on coatings and even tougher on exposed wood; so, if you live in a hot, humid part of the country, choose paint over stain.

Surface Preparation

The first step of prep work is to closely inspect the house. If there is peeling paint, why is it peeling? Was the peeling caused by a gutter or roof leak? Is the paint peeling down to the primer, or is the primer popping off as well? Is there mildew on the house?

The quality of a paint job can be no better than the quality of the prep work. For a paint job to be successful, problems such as leaks must be cured; damaged wood must be repaired; loose paint must be removed; and, the surface must be cleaned. Good prep virtually guarantees a good paint job.

Blistering & Peeling

Blistered paint looks as if it has bubbled from the surface, while peeling paint comes off in sheets. Both problems are usually caused by water. In the case of blistering, the paint could have been applied over a damp, oily or dirty surface; or water vapor may be migrating out of the interior of the house. This typically happens around kitchens, bathrooms and laundry rooms.

Paint usually peels because the wood behind it has swelled. Again, water vapor from inside the house can be the problem. The most likely problem is a roof or gutter leak that concentrates water on the peeled area.

Insulation that has been added to exterior walls without the benefit of a complete vapor barrier inside may cause peeling. Interior moisture that once migrated harmlessly through the walls condenses inside, causing the siding to swell. (This problem also can cause rot within the walls.)

In colder parts of the country ice dams formed at the edge of the roof cause leaks in the walls. This too, results in peeling paint. Ice dams are cured with specialized roofing techniques, or by installation of heat tape that prevents ice dams from forming.

Older houses with many coats of paint sometimes peel after receiving a fresh coat of paint. If paint layers have built up to a "critical mass," one more coat is often enough to break the weak bond between the paint and the wood underneath. There is no reliable test for critical mass, but if the paint is starting to alligator, you can be sure it is not far away.

Isolate the cause of blistering and peeling, and cure it before priming or painting. Use a hand scraper to remove peeled or blistered paint, exposing a sound surface that takes the new paint. If you are not sure about your diagnosis of the problem, talk to the salespeople at a good paint store.

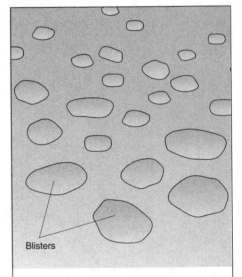

Blisters

Blistering and Peeling.
Blistering and peeling is often caused by poor preparation or moisture leakage.

Alligatoring & Checking

Alligatored paint, true to its name, looks like alligator skin. Checking is essentially the same thing, only the paint film is more deeply cracked. Alligatored paint is caused by paint that is applied too thickly; paint that dries too quickly (most likely on a hot day or in direct sun); or a second coat of paint that is applied before the first coat is dry. On older houses, it can occur simply because paint shrinks and cracks with age.

To avoid alligatored paint apply thin coats, and do not paint in the direct sun on a hot day.

If the house is old and the paint is thick, alligatored areas must be stripped before the new paint is applied. Remove loose, checked paint with a hand scraper. If you find yourself with a big stripping job, consider hiring a professional. A whole-house stripping job is time-consuming, dirty, and may require the use of toxic chemicals (which require specialized protective and cleanup equipment). For more on stripping, see pages 34-36.

Chalking

When paint film starts to break down, it decomposes into a layer of fine dust. Light-colored stains often are visible on a brick house, under painted areas that have started to chalk. Run your hand over the paint. If you pick up a layer of light-colored dust, then the paint is chalking. Before primer or paint is applied, the residue must be scrubbed with trisodium phosphate (TSP), followed by a thorough pressure-washing. Trisodium phosphate is a strong cleaner, available at most paint stores.

Removing Paint

There are many ways to "skin" the house. Peeling and cracking paint must be removed before the primer and new paint go on. The condition of the existing paint, the extent of any problems, tools on hand, and your

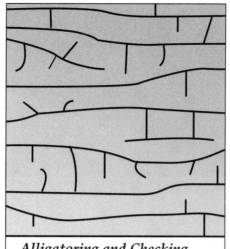

Alligatoring and Checking. Alligatored paint is caused by paint that was applied too thickly or dried too quickly. Sometimes the cause is simply age.

own inclinations help decide the best way to remove problem paint.

When scraping, sanding or stripping, remember this: If the paint is stuck tight enough to resist reasonable efforts to remove it, then it is not going to fall off anytime soon. Just leave it in place.

Scraping Paint

Scraping is the easiest, least toxic, and lowest-tech way to remove problem paint. This method is labor intensive but for the homeowner it is simple, fairly tidy and definitely the best way to go for most paint removal.

The best tool for the job is a pull scraper, which has a big knob over the blade end, and removable blades. Be sure to buy plenty of replacement blades if you have a lot scraping to do. The blades dull quickly, and you will change them fairly often. When using a pull scraper, keep the blade flat on the surface. If you rotate the scraper, the edge of the blade digs in and scars the wood.

Caution: *Wear eye protection and gloves when scraping.*

Because you cannot get as much downward pressure on them, push

scrapers tend to remove less paint. However, they are handy when using a heat gun because they require only one hand. You can run the heat gun just ahead of the scraper which easily lifts the softened paint. It might be good to have one on hand just to give your pulling muscles an occasional break. One advantage to using push scrapers is that they send the chips flying away from you.

If your house has highly-detailed molding, such as dentil, egg-and-dart trim or highly ornate window and door casings you need molding scrapers. Molding scrapers come in shapes that match common molding profiles and usually are available at well-stocked paint stores and home center stores.

The main pitfall of hand scraping is damaging the wood. Pull scrapers tend to dig in at the edge, making gashes in the wood that must be patched before the house is painted. Push scrapers break out corners of molding. The work is also time-consuming and hard physically, even though it is the safest and cleanest way to remove problem paint.

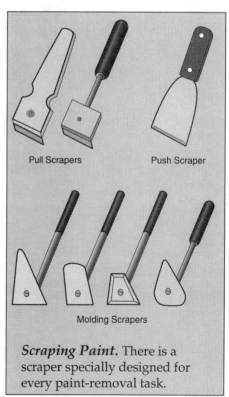

Pull Scrapers

Push Scraper

Molding Scrapers

Scraping Paint. There is a scraper specially designed for every paint-removal task.

The following is a list of the basic safety tools you will need for a scraping job.

■ A pair of heavy gloves and a long-sleeved shirt. If the blade slips, your hands and arms are protected.

■ A dust mask. A paper mask rated for nuisance dust is often sufficient. However, houses painted before the mid 1970s are likely to have some lead-based paint. If you have much scraping to do on an older house, use a respirator rated for lead-laced dust (ask your respirator supplier for the proper mask). If you wear a respirator, bear in mind that breathing, and the work, will take more effort. If you have heart or respiratory problems, check with your physician before exerting yourself while wearing a respirator.

■ Eye protection. Wear safety glasses, or better yet, goggles. Goggles afford better eye protection, but they also tend to fog up.

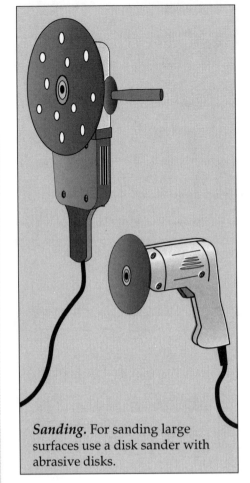

Sanding. For sanding large surfaces use a disk sander with abrasive disks.

Sanding

If your house suffers from large areas of peeling, alligatored or blistering paint, or if there are many layers of paint to remove, sanding may be the best option. Sanding is the quickest way to get shingles or clapboards down to bare wood. Do not try to do the job with a sanding attachment for your power drill. You need a rotary disk sander, sometimes called a disk grinder. This is a heavy-duty, two-handed machine. Use paper or fiber-backed sanding disks. You can buy the sander and disks at paint stores and home center stores.

Sanding is quick and effective but it is hard, messy work. Dust is the biggest problem. Of course you need to put down drop cloths, but dust still swirls and blows around in the wind. Some sanders come with collection bags but if you use one of these, be wary of striking a nail

head, creating a spark, and in turn causing a flash fire.

Caution: *Always wear long pants and sleeves as chips fly off at a surprising rate. Wear eye protection and gloves for the same reason. If the house was painted before the late 1970s, there is a good chance that some of the dust contains lead. It is therefore essential to have the proper respiratory protection. Buy a mask with replaceable cartridges that allow for exhalation. A paper nuisance mask is not sufficient. Some municipalities forbid sanding because of lead problems, so check local standards.*

Most jobs need to be sanded twice. Use 16-grit disks for aggressive paint removal. Then give the surfaces a quick light pass with 60-grit sandpaper to smooth it enough for painting. Powerful sanders sometimes leave permanent marks on the surface. Keep a sander moving and do not dwell on one area, or the sander dishes out the wood and creates a recessed semi-circular pattern that the paint highlights. Also, resist the temptation to turn the sander at an angle. This seems to take paint off faster, but in fact creates gouges in the wood. Keep the sanding disk parallel to the surface at all times.

1 **Preparing to Sand.** Close all windows on the side of the house being sanded. Lay heavy drop cloths to catch most of the chips and dust. Ensure that all power cords are untangled and have sufficient length.

2 **Beginning to Sand.** Turn the sander on. Lower the disk carefully onto the siding as high as you can comfortably reach. Do not stretch, you will not be able to control the sander. Keep the sander moving horizontally while applying light, constant pressure. Sand as much as you can comfortably reach to both sides until bare wood is exposed.

1 Proper preparation makes cleaning after sanding much easier. Lay drop cloths to catch the dust. Make sure cords are untangled and long enough.

Disc Sander

2 Lower the spinning sander on the wood and sand as high as you can comfortably reach.

3 Keep the sander moving left and right as you work down the surface of the siding.

4 Hold the sander with the disk facing up to sand the bottom edge of clapboard or shingles.

Molding Scraper

5 Use a molding scraper to remove paint where the rotary sander cannot reach.

3 Moving Down. Once the wood on top is bare, move down without stopping or turning the disk at an angle. Again work left and right as far as you can comfortably reach.

4 Sanding the Lip. If there is much paint build-up, you need to sand the bottom edge of clapboards or siding. Do this by turning the sander at a 90-degree angle to the siding. Use a very light touch. You are sanding a very small surface with a lot of sander and you can chew off a noticeable chunk of siding before you realize it.

5 Scraping the Corners. The sanding disk will not reach into corners where siding meets vertical trim. In most cases, the easiest way to remove this paint is with a molding scraper. If caulking between siding and trim is dried out, scrape it out at this time.

Stripping Paint

Stripping is another alternative for paint removal. The good thing about stripping is that it removes paint down to the original surface. After painting, the stripped wood looks like new again. However, there are a few bad consequences of stripping paint: It is messy, time-consuming, labor-intensive work, and the most effective paint strippers are toxic. Stripping a door, or molding that lost its detail to built-up paint is one thing, while stripping a whole house is something else. If you have to strip the exterior, work on a small section and keep track of the time and effort you spend on the job. If the scope of the whole job appears to be overwhelming, consider hiring a professional. Specialized contractors can use proprietary chemical stripping methods to strip an entire house.

A professional might use any number of methods to strip a house. Heat stripping is the low-tech, least toxic method. Chemical stripping can be a brush-on, scrape-off method; or a proprietary method in which the areas to be stripped are wrapped with a paint-removing poultice. To decide on a paint-stripping contractor, ask for and check the company's references. If your house is very old, check with local historical societies for companies that specialize in stripping old buildings.

Stripping Paint with Heat

For most exterior stripping projects, heat stripping is the way to go. Years ago, painters used blowtorches to strip houses. They simply turned the torch on the paint until it bubbled, and then they scraped it off. There are two problems with this approach: First, more than a few houses were burned down this way. Blowtorches easily ignite wood and hidden debris such as a bird's nest. Second, the heat from a blowtorch volatilizes lead in lead-based paint, producing a toxic gas. Simply put, do not strip paint with a blowtorch, and do not let anybody else do it on your house.

These days, there are two good tools for heat stripping: the heat gun and the heat plate. Heat guns are best for uneven surfaces, such as trim and molding. Heat plates make fast work of flat surfaces, such as siding. While these tools generate enough heat to set wood or hidden debris afire, they pose much less risk than using a blowtorch.

Caution: *Wear gloves, long sleeves and pants to protect yourself while you work. Heat stripping creates big, crunchy paint chips. The chips are hot when they fall away from the surface, so keep children and pets away from the job. When stripping outside, lay heavy canvas drop cloths to catch chips that might otherwise be pushed into the ground.*

At the end of every work session, sweep or vacuum up the chips and dispose of them properly. (The chips may contain lead.)

Use a push scraper for most heat stripping. When stripping paint from molding, use a molding scraper that conforms to the ins and outs of the molding. (These are available at most paint and hardware stores.) Ingenious practitioners have gone so far as to use old spoons and dental picks as molding scrapers.

Using Heat Guns. Heat guns are essentially industrial-strength blow dryers. They vary widely in quality. At the low end are inexpensive heat guns which can be found in hardware stores and home center stores. These guns are good for light-duty work, as long as you do not drop them. Most inexpensive heat guns cannot be repaired. When the heating element or blower motor burns out or breaks, the gun is useless.

There are medium-quality guns that are a little sturdier than the cheapest guns, but most cannot be repaired.

At the high end, there are industrial quality guns, which can cost more than 100 dollars. If you have much stripping to do, and you can afford one of these, buy one. A professional quality gun is much sturdier than a cheaper model, and it will survive most drops intact. Replacement parts are sold for these types of guns.

Using Heat Guns. This tool strips paint on both flat surfaces and detailed molding.

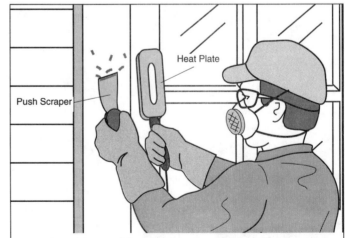

Using a Heat Plate. This is a safe paint removal method and works best on flat surfaces.

Caution: *A heat gun does not remove paint from brick or metal. These materials simply absorb the heat, and have to be chemically stripped. Heat-stripping is for wood. If you have vinyl siding on your house, keep the heat gun away from it. A heat gun melts vinyl siding.*

During heat stripping, hot paint chips fly, so wear a long-sleeved shirt and heavy gloves. Although heat guns generally do not get paint hot enough to volatilize lead, it can happen, so wear a mask or respirator rated for toxic fumes.

Using a heat gun is fairly straightforward. Hold the gun a few inches away from the paint you want to strip, and move the gun over a small area. When the paint bubbles, scrape it off with a push scraper. Keep the gun moving. Be careful not to ignite the paint or scorch the underlying wood. If you do scorch the wood, sand it down until you come to good wood.

Be careful not to direct the hot air from the heat gun into any openings in the house. Small openings are often home to wasps and birds, both of which make flammable nests. Keep a fire extinguisher handy as you work, and stay at the job site for an hour or so after you finish to ensure that no smoldering fires catch.

Once the chips of paint cool off, sweep them up. Remember, they might contain lead, so check with local waste disposal authorities for rules and regulations on their disposal.

Using a Heat Plate. A heat plate is essentially a heating element, with a metal cover over it, attached to a handle. A heat plate is the fastest tool for heat-stripping large expanses of flat surface. Heat plates cost less than heat guns. Precautions for the heat plate are the same as for the heat gun. Wear protective clothing, and do not direct the heat into openings on the house. Heat plates, having no blowers, are much less likely than heat guns to start a fire in a hidden cavity.

Hold the heat plate on, or an inch or two above, the paint. Wait until the paint bubbles, and scrape it off. As with the heat gun, be careful not to ignite the paint or scorch the underlying wood. Sand and prime any areas that become scorched.

Stripping Paint Chemically

Chemically stripping a large area is a big, messy, expensive job. For the best combination of stripping and safety, use a paste stripper that contains methylene chloride.

Caution: *Methylene chloride is thought to be carcinogenic, so wear a mask rated for toxic fumes. Less expensive, and less effective strippers, are strongly alkaline, and can cause nasty burns. Eye protection is a must when using chemical strippers—they can literally blind a person. Wear an old long-sleeve shirt and heavy gloves with the understanding that the clothing and gloves will be thrown away when the job is done.*

Strippers advertised as "safe" are still powerful stuff. While less toxic than the methylene chloride strippers, they do not work nearly as well.

There are proprietary whole-house chemical stripping systems that are available to specialized contractors. The most common one has stripper embedded in a sort of plastic-covered poultice, which is applied over the area to be stripped. When the poultice comes off, so does the paint (most of it anyway). This kind of job is neat compared to a do-it-yourself job. Consider hiring a contractor who does this type of work.

Spatters of chemical stripper take the paint off anything they touch. Careful masking is also a must. Use heavy canvas drop cloths (thin plastic drop cloths melt in the places stripper falls).

Following Directions

Each stripper is formulated differently so follow the directions on the container. A few commonalities apply to almost all chemical strippers: They do not work in cold weather. Because the strippers work chemically, the hotter the weather the better. Do not consider chemical stripping until the weather reaches the mid 70s. Most strippers must be neutralized either with water or alcohol before the surface accepts paint again. Read the container directions carefully.

Regardless of the type of chemical stripper, the job involves using a disposable brush to apply stripper liberally, waiting a few minutes for the stripper to work, then scraping off the paint. Depending on the quality of the stripper, the temperature, and the dwell time (elapsed time of stripper on the surface), the process might have to be repeated.

1 Laying on the Stripper. Using an old brush (do not use a foam brush, it will melt), liberally apply chemical stripper. Do not brush out the stripper as you would paint. Just lay it on roughly, and leave it.

1 Use an old, throw-away bristle brush to lay the stripper on the surface. Do not brush the stripper out, just let it work.

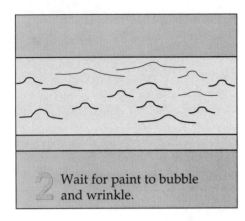

2 Wait for paint to bubble and wrinkle.

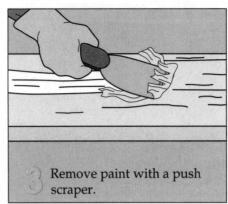

3 Remove paint with a push scraper.

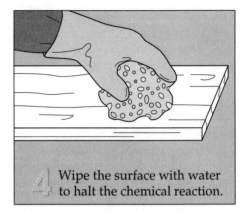

4 Wipe the surface with water to halt the chemical reaction.

2 Waiting for Chemical Reaction. This is an easy step, but an important one. Give the stripper time to make all the paint bubble away from the surface. This usually takes about 10 minutes.

3 Removing the Paint. Using a push scraper, remove the paint from the surface. Use coarse steel wool to remove stripper from curved areas such as moldings. Repeat Steps 1 through 3, as necessary.

4 Neutralizing the Stripper. Wipe down the stripped surface with clear water, or with alcohol if specified on the container.

Caulking

Caulking is an essential part of the prep work for an exterior paint job. Besides preventing air leaks around windows, doors, and construction joints, caulk keeps water out. Caulk is also known as "carpenter's helper" because it fills in cracks and gives a seamless appearance to woodwork.

Silicone caulk is expensive, but gives the best performance. A high-quality silicone caulk withstands temperature and humidity changes better than other types. The one disadvantage to using silicone caulk is that it cannot be painted. For this

reason, it is best to save silicone for joints that are not readily visible.

For joints that are to be painted, the best choices are latex and acrylic caulks. These caulks are a little cheaper than silicone caulk, and they work well and take paint well.

Repairing Damaged Wood

Damaged wood is always repaired as part of the prep work. No paint job looks good applied over damaged wood, and if the wood is water-damaged, the paint most likely will not adhere to the surface.

Caulking. Caulk open joints with paintable caulk. Let caulk cure completely before painting.

Caulk Gun

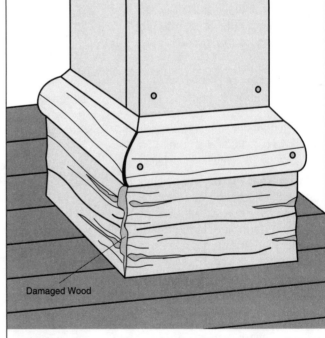

Repairing Damaged Wood. Damaged wood is repaired with epoxy after the cause of the damage is eliminated.

Damaged Wood

Before repairing water-damaged wood, be sure to locate the source of the water and eliminate it. Leaky gutters and downspouts are frequent offenders. Some wood pieces, such as modern window sills and some moldings, are available in stock sizes. Stock materials often can be replaced more easily than they can be repaired.

Epoxy

1 Use an old putty knife to mix epoxy according to the directions on the can.

Damaged wood can be repaired in place by patching. Many exterior patching products are available, including exterior spackling and wood putty. The best materials for exterior patching, although a bit on the expensive side, are two-part epoxies (available at well-stocked paint stores and home center stores). Even severely damaged wood can be repaired this way. These proprietary, two-step systems consist of a thin liquid that is poured onto damaged wood to harden it; followed by a patch made of two-part epoxy. Epoxy patches can be sanded, drilled and worked with power tools. Generally, the epoxy patch is stronger than the surrounding wood. Epoxy patches are primed and painted just like wood.

If you have ornate, or unique features such as old moldings, window and door surrounds, or column bases, have them repaired by a good finish carpenter. It is too difficult to learn finish carpentry just to do the prep work for one paint job.

1 **Mixing the Epoxy.** Thoroughly mix the parts according to the manufacturer's instructions—typically one part resin to one part hardener. Mix on a board, not in a container. Epoxy works by a heat reaction. If you mix too much of it in a small container the heat may build up to a point where it ruins the epoxy before you get a chance to use it.

2 **Applying the Epoxy.** With a putty knife, apply the epoxy patching material. Work quickly. Once the epoxy starts to harden, you will not be able to spread it. Use a putty knife to work the epoxy into shape to match the damaged piece. When the epoxy starts to harden, stop working.

3 **Shaping the Epoxy** When the epoxy is cured, sand it into shape. You can also shape it quite successfully with a wood chisel.

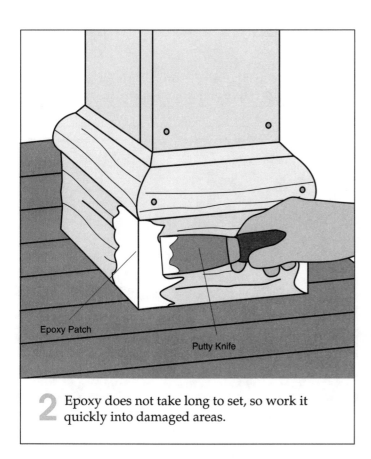

Epoxy Patch

Putty Knife

2 Epoxy does not take long to set, so work it quickly into damaged areas.

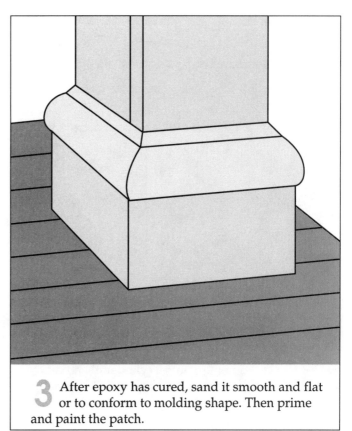

3 After epoxy has cured, sand it smooth and flat or to conform to molding shape. Then prime and paint the patch.

Repairing Windows

Before repainting, closely inspect the windows for loose glazing putty. If you find any, it will have to be removed and replaced.

1 **Removing Loose Putty.** Use a molding scraper to scrape out the old putty. Stubborn putty can be removed by heating it. Use an electric soldering iron applied directly to the putty. (Do not use a heat gun—the blast of hot air can cause window glass to break.) Do not obsess over removing the last dregs of putty. If it is stuck tight, it does not need to come off. If the scraper does not move, it might be caught on a glazing point, not loose putty. Glazing points are little metal triangles pushed into the sides of the muntins to help hold the glass in place.

2 **Cleaning the Surface.** Brush out pieces of dust and dirt from the window muntins to provide a clean surface. Replace glass and secure with glazing points.

3 **Placing the Putty.** Replace damaged putty with new glazing putty. Pull the putty out of the can with your hand and roll it into a cylinder that is roughly the diameter of a pencil. If the putty sticks to your hands, put a little linseed oil on your hands before working it. If the putty crumbles, it has dried out and you need to get fresh material. Place the putty on the windows, squeezing it against the muntins and the glass.

4 **Shaping the Putty.** Dip a putty knife in linseed oil to prevent sticking. Place the knife at a 45-degree angle to the window glass, then pull the knife across in one stroke, forming a seal. This is a warm weather job; cold glazing putty does not form.

Molding Scraper

Glazing Putty

1 Use a molding scraper to work out old window glazing putty.

2 Be sure to clean all dirt and debris off window muntins before reglazing. Replace glass.

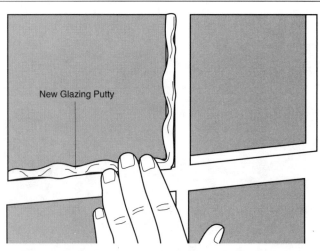

New Glazing Putty

3 Roll glazing putty into a cylinder, then press onto the muntin. Glazing extends 3/8-inch up on window glass.

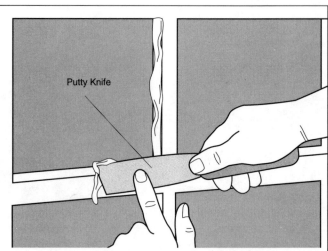

Putty Knife

4 Draw putty knife across the new putty at a 45-degree angle. At the corner draw the knife sharply away from the window. Let putty cure before painting.

Preparing to Prime. While wearing eye protection and rubber gloves, wash dirt and grit off the house with TSP and water solution. Scrub the surface with a brush attached to a pole.

Preparing to Prime

Before the house is primed or repainted, it must be thoroughly cleaned to remove dirt, grease and chalking. As noted earlier, a professional house-washing contractor is often the easiest and best way to go. If you do it yourself, the simplest and best way is by hand washing. Use a solution of trisodium phosphate (TSP), available at paint stores. Put on rubber gloves and goggles, and with a scrub brush attached to a pole, wash down the exterior surfaces. Rinse the house with a garden hose and then rinse off plants below, to keep them from being burned by the TSP solution.

This job is done more quickly with a pressure washer, which is avail-able at most rental supply houses. However, these tools can be troublesome and even dangerous. They can blow out mortar, drive water into and through walls, and propel a person off a ladder. If you want the house pressure washed, hire a professional who has insurance. If you want to do the job yourself, stick to hand washing.

Exterior Primers & Sealers

Priming is not so much the first coat of paint, as it is the last step of preparation. Primer allows the finish paint to stick—and stay stuck—to the painted surface. Primer also keeps stains, such as turpentine that weeps out of knots in wood, from bleeding through the finish coats. Match primer to the material to be painted. A good wood primer is not necessarily a good metal primer. To make sure you get the right primer, ask for advice at a paint store. Make sure you read the directions and specifications on the label.

Using Wood Primer

Exterior wood, plywood or hardboard must be primed with latex or oil-based wood primer. As with finish paint, latex primers can be cleaned up with soap and water, while oil-based primers must be cleaned up with solvents such as mineral spirits.

Oil-based primer has a moderate advantage in its ability to hold out stains, such as the turpentine that weeps from knots in wood. However, oil primer tends to pop off wet wood. If water gets between the wood and the primer (one common source is vapor drive—water vapor that migrates out from the house), oil primer loses its bond, causing the paint to peel down to the bare wood.

Latex primers are fairly tolerant of vapor drive. There are two disadvantages to using latex primers: latex-primed surfaces sometimes require an extra topcoat; and latex primer sometimes allows rust stains from nail heads to show through the finish paint. (Yes, even if a builder uses hot-dipped galvanized nails on exterior surfaces, the rust-resistant coating takes a beating from hammers and nail guns.) If the wood is unpainted, or if rust stains show through, spot-prime nail heads with an oil- or shellac-based primer.

Using Metal Primers

Most people think that ferrous metals, such as iron and steel, and commonly used flashings such as terne and galvanized steel, must be painted, while aluminum and copper do not require painting. It is true that ferrous metals (coated metal such as terne metal and galvanized steel included) have to be painted; but it is not necessarily true that aluminum or copper do not need to be painted. Aluminum corrodes if left unpainted. It lasts longer and looks better when painted. Copper does not rust if left unpainted, but the greenish runoff from copper roofing and flashing stains surfaces below. Painting the copper takes care of this problem.

Ferrous Metal Primers. Ferrous metal is iron-bearing metal; that is, iron and steel. Galvanized steel, commonly used for gutters and flashings, is a ferrous metal. There are three types of ferrous metal primers: bright metal primer, rusty metal primer and rust converters.

Use bright metal primer for new metal, or for newly-prepped metal that has been sanded to remove rust. Use rusty metal primer if the metal shows some surface rust. (Of course, all loose rust has to be removed with a wire brush before the metal is primed.) Rust converters promote a chemical reaction that arrests rusting, but they cannot work miracles. Very rusty metal needs replacing and no paint will help.

Before priming galvanized steel, wipe it down with mineral spirits to remove the factory-applied coating of oil. Then, use a primer specifically suited to galvanized steel.

Never use aluminum paint (the shiny silver stuff) on ferrous metals. Aluminum-to-steel contact sets up galvanic corrosion, which slowly destroys the ferrous metal.

Aluminum Primers. Aluminum is primed with a latex metal primer, or an oil-based zinc chromate paint. Top-coat aluminum with ordinary latex house paint.

If you are painting aluminum gutters, make sure there is no standing water left inside. Gutters that require painting need to be painted on the inside too.

Covering the Primer

As a general rule, the faster the primer dries, the sooner you have to repaint. No primer does its job if it is left exposed indefinitely. If the primer is allowed to weather beyond a critical point, it will fail, or will cure so hard that the top coat cannot stick to it. Read the manufacturer's label specifications for the optimum time between priming and applying the topcoat. With some primers, you can recoat in a matter of hours. With others, you can wait a few weeks. Whatever you do, do not prime in the spring and plan to finish painting in the fall. You will end up redoing the entire job.

Painting Sequence

Circumstance has a lot to do with determining your painting sequence, and personal preference plays a role too. For example, on summer days

---

Terne Metal

The material that most people call "roofing tin" is actually terne metal. Terne (French for "dull") is steel, covered with a combination lead and tin coating. It is manufactured by Follansbee Steel, in Follansbee, West Virginia. Terne has been used as a roofing and flashing material since the earliest days of the Republic, and properly painted, it can last virtually forever. However, improperly painted, it self-destructs. If you have a terne metal roof or terne metal flashing, follow Follansbee's recommendations for prepping, priming and painting. Coatings such as roofing tar and aluminum paint actually hasten the destruction of the metal.

---

you will want to plan a strategy that keeps you out of the sun. If you are right-handed, work from left to right. If you are left-handed, work from right to left.

Working from the Top Down. When painting outside, work from the top down. There are two reasons for this: The first is the standing construction-trades rule about doing the hard work first, when concentration is best and before fatigue sets in. Second, paint drips down, so you can remove drips as you proceed with the job.

Working Horizontally. Work horizontally to visual break points. For instance, finish off a whole window surround, or work to the end of a wall. Plan your workday so that you make it to a break point before quitting time.

When working horizontally on a ladder, do not even consider scooting the ladder over as you stand on it. Always climb down and move the ladder to the next area, making sure the ladder is stable and level before going back up.

Painting the Siding First. Start at the peak of a gable end. Set up ladders and ladder jacks (if needed). When you have finished the siding on one gable end, paint the trim on that end to minimize ladder movement. When you have finished one gable repeat the sequence for the other gable. Then move on to the remaining sides of the house.

Painting Downstairs Doors and Windows. Plan your work so you paint downstairs doors and windows early in the day. That way, they will be dry at the end of the workday, allowing you to reinstall hardware and lock up ground floor doors and windows at night.

Painting Siding

Painting Lapped Siding

Use as large a brush as you can comfortably handle. A four-inch brush is a good choice.

1 Painting Bottom Edges. Paint the bottom edges of siding first, laying on the paint and then brushing out.

2 Painting the Face. Lay paint on the face of the siding, covering as large an area as you can brush out before the paint starts to pull. Brush the paint out using horizontal strokes (on shingles brush vertically along with the grain of the wood). Keep a wet edge and work to a logical stopping point (the end of a wall or a window or door frame). Drips often form on the bottom edges of siding, so be sure to look back over the work from time to time, to pick up any drips or runs.

1 Start painting at the bottom edge of a course.

2 Lay paint on and brush along with the wood grain. Brush strokes are horizontal for clapboard, vertical for shingles.

Tips for Spraying

Here are a few tips to remember if you decide to use spray equipment to paint the siding:

■ Always wear eye and respiratory protection when spraying. The mist is fine and can be irritating and potentially harmful.

■ Be aware that the tiny paint droplets are apt to drift in the air. They can land on neighbors' houses, cars, foliage, and driveways causing big problems. Never spray on windy days. When working on corners, spray vertically to avoid over-spray which can ruin a roof. Stop spraying about two feet short of all edges and brush paint on.

■ Good technique involves a steady wrist making quick and sure spray passes. Do not throw your arm out in an arc. Every sprayer concentrates the paint in the middle of the swath emitted so you must feather the edges of every swath about one third of the way into the previous pass to ensure an even coat of paint. Do not stop your hand or

hold the trigger too long because too much paint will come out.

■ Most paint is too thick to pour directly from the can into the sprayer. Mix paint with an appropriate solvent (water or oil-based) to allow proper misting.

■ Never allow debris to get into the sprayer. The paint pot or connector tube must have a wire mesh cover to prevent objects from getting sucked in. When using previously opened paint be sure to strain the paint through cheesecloth or panty hose to remove particles.

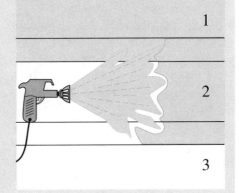

Painting Plywood and Grooved Siding. Use a roller on plywood siding then brush in missed spots.

Painting Plywood & Grooved Siding

Paint Texture-1-11 (T-1-11) plywood siding using a long-nap roller. Use a brush for cutting in (painting areas where the roller does not reach or where you want a sharply defined color change). Keep the brush handy as you roll on the paint. Switch to the brush frequently, brushing paint evenly into vertical grooves.

Working with Masonry

Painting Brick

Do not paint brick unless it has already been painted. Unlike wood, brick does not need to be painted to survive the weather. (The one exception to this rule applies to brick that has been sandblasted. In this case, the brick is painted with latex to prevent water from seeping into the walls.) In fact, brick survives best unpainted because the hard face of the brick is tougher than paint, and peeling paint tends to trap moisture in the mortar. Once brick is painted, you are stuck with the ongoing maintenance of keeping it painted. If the brick is dirty, have it cleaned. Even the dirtiest brick can be cleaned so it looks brand new. Cleaning brick often costs less than painting it and the cleaning lasts a lot longer than a paint job. Brick by itself does not require cleaning but once every fifty years. The best contractor for the job is one who has experience cleaning older buildings.

Never sandblast or blast with any other abrasive. Sandblasting destroys the hard face of the brick, and allows water penetration, which destroys brick.

Before painting brick, have cracks repointed (mortared). Apply latex paint with a long-nap roller, switching frequently to a brush to work paint into the mortar joints. Check the work frequently, and pick up runs or drips.

The above instructions apply to concrete block as well.

Painting Stucco

Stucco is painted using latex paint applied with a long-nap roller. However, unlike siding and other surfaces with many plane changes, stucco is an ideal surface for spraying. If you have an airless sprayer, cut-in inside corners with a brush, then spray.

1 **Making Repairs.** Patch any cracks or bulges in stucco before repainting. Make sure there are no cracks in windows, door sills or coping that allows water to penetrate the stucco. If cracks are present, patch with stucco or a caulk that can be painted.

2 **Priming Stucco.** Prime stucco with a latex primer before painting. This is important because patches that have not been primed have different textures and absorption rates and cause an obvious change of gloss in the finish paint.

3 **Painting Stucco.** Paint stucco with latex paint, using a long-nap roller. The heavier the texture of the stucco, the more you have to brush out uneven areas, runs and drips.

1 Before painting stucco all holes and cracks must be patched. A professional can match stucco textures.

2 Prime stucco with a latex primer to avoid flashing.

3 Finish painting stucco with a long-nap roller.

INTERIOR PAINTING

The key to a good paint job is preparation. In fact, about 80 percent of a painting job consists of preparation, while only 20 percent of the work is painting. When the job is finished, the paint itself is not as noticeable as the care taken during the preparation work.

Getting Started

In a new house wall and ceiling surfaces are in excellent condition, so you can expect only two to three hours of prep time for every hour spent painting. On the other hand, in an older home which most likely has some cracked plaster or paint buildup on the trim, it is not unusual to spend eight to ten hours prepping to every hour spent painting. If the job requires layers of patching, ample drying time must be provided, so plan ahead.

Organizing the Room

If it is possible to remove all of the furniture from the room, do so. It is easier to move the furniture than it is to work around it. If some furniture must remain in the room, leave at least four feet of open space along the walls, and make sure you can reach the entire ceiling.

Removing Hardware. Doorknobs, escutcheons, window locks and curtain rods must be removed. If the screws on any of this hardware are worn, now is the time to buy replacements. If standardized hardware, such as a window lock, is paint-encrusted or damaged, it might be easier to install replacement hardware than to clean up the existing material. However, you probably want to save and clean antique hardware if at all possible.

Storing Hardware. Put the hardware in plastic bags, so you do not lose or mix up parts. Use common masking tape, available at any paint or hardware store, to mask hardware that must stay in place (such as door hinges).

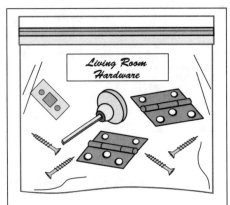

Storing Hardware. Store small hardware in zip-lock plastic bags. Label the bags to keep hardware coordinated with its location.

Removing Switch and Outlet Covers. If they are modern standardized parts, replace any paint-encrusted or damaged pieces.

Covering Ceiling Fixtures. Carefully mask ceiling fixtures. Put an old sheet or plastic sheeting, over chandeliers and ceiling fans. It is much easier to paint the ceiling if you unscrew the ring at the top of the chandelier and allow the canopy to slide down toward the light.

Cleaning Brass Hardware

Place hardware in an enameled pan with a solution of baking soda and water. Use about four tablespoons of baking soda per quart of water. Simmer the solution on top of a stove until the paint softens. Dump the hardware out of the pan, let it cool enough to touch, and then take off the paint with a stiff bristle brush or toothbrush (not a wire brush). Polish the hardware with brass polish.

Tips for Buying Drop Cloths

Drop cloths are an important part of the job. Many do-it-yourselfers try to get by with makeshift drop cloths, and the results often show. It is best to buy good-quality fabric drop cloths. Canvas drop cloths do the best job and last a lifetime, but they are not inexpensive. Avoid the temptation to use inexpensive plastic drop cloths on the floor. Plastic is slick to walk on, and shreds under foot traffic.

Discarded bed sheets work fairly well, especially for covering furniture, chandeliers or ceiling fans. Old sheets protect objects from the roller's spray, but drops of paint run right through them.

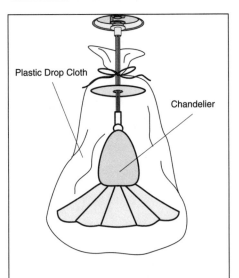

Covering Ceiling Fixtures. "Bag" chandeliers with a piece of plastic drop cloth.

Covering Up. Place drop cloths over furniture left in the room (if any). Mask the trim that you do not plan to repaint (such as baseboards, and door and window trim). Place drop cloths or roll kraft paper over the floor and tape it at the seams and edges. Be sure to use painter's masking tape—duct tape and regular masking tape is too sticky and removes surfaces if left in place for a few days.

Repairing Minor Flaws & Damage

Walls are subject to a variety of assaults that damage their surface, especially in a house with children. Besides the everyday wear and tear of impact and gouges, walls also develop cracks as the house settles. Before beginning any paint job, study the surfaces carefully and make the necessary repairs.

Filling Nail Holes & Cracks

Nail holes and hairline cracks are filled with spackling compound or drywall compound (often called drywall mud). Spackling compound is available in small containers, while drywall compound is generally available in quarts or five-gallon buckets. If the walls require minimal preparation (such as filling nail holes), choose a quick-drying spackling compound that has very little shrinkage and can be painted in as little as 10-15 minutes.

Both compounds are applied with a putty knife and sanded with 100-grit sandpaper when dry.

Feathering the Edges. To make sure a patch is not readily apparent it must be "feathered." This term refers to the technique of tapering and sanding the edges of a patch into a very gradual slope. You cannot feel a ridge at the edge of a patch that is properly feathered.

Patching Splits, Dents, Gaps. Minor nicks and dents in woodwork and trim are patched with wood filler, spackling compound or drywall compound. If yours is a fairly modern house, and replacement wood trim is readily available, it may be easier to replace heavily damaged trim than to patch it. For older houses, especially those with distinctive trim, it is always worth the effort to restore damaged parts. However, often times these types of restorations require skills you may not possess, such as finish carpentry, wood finishing, and simple carving. Consider hiring a professional if you are unsure of your skills.

Patch nicks and dents with wood filler, spreading the filler with a putty knife, or if necessary, your finger. Fingers are often the best smoothing tool, but if you use them work slowly to avoid splinters. Overfill nicks and dents slightly. When the filler cures, use 100-grit sandpaper to sand it flush with the wood surface.

Fill gaps at corners and between trim and wall surfaces with a high-quality caulk that takes paint. Again, your water-dampened finger is often the best smoothing tool (water keeps the caulk from sticking to your finger). Use a damp cloth to clean up any stray caulk. Do not try to sand caulk; it rolls under sandpaper. To get a sharp edge on a bead of caulk, trim it with a craft knife. Let caulk dry thoroughly before priming or painting.

Drywall Joint

Drywall Tape

Drywall Compound

Feathering the Edges. The patch edges are tapered and sanded or "feathered" until smooth.

Patching Splits, Dents, Gaps. If modern trim is significantly damaged, it might be easier to replace it than to repair it. High-quality antique features are worth restoring.

Repairing Holes in Plaster

Before World War II and well into the 1950s most walls and ceilings were comprised of three coats of plaster applied over wood lath. The material used for almost all walls and ceilings built after World War II is drywall.

While the methods for repairing minor flaws and nail holes is the same for both types of wall, the methods differ for bigger repairs.

Holes in plaster that are no bigger than a fist can be patched with drywall compound as long as the lath behind the hole is still intact. Drywall compound tends to crack when used for larger holes.

1 **Spraying the Lath.** Using a spray bottle, spray exposed wood lath with water until the lath is just damp.

2 **Applying Layers of Drywall Compound.** Apply a 1/4-inch layer of compound (do not worry about making this layer smooth). When the layer is dry, apply one or two more 1/4-inch layers, allowing each coat to dry thoroughly, until the patch is flush with the wall. When the patch is dry, apply a final layer and let it dry.

3 **Feathering the Edges.** Use fine sandpaper or a wet sanding sponge to feather the edges of the patch over the sound plaster. A sanding sponge is a rectangular sponge with one rough side. Dust stays on the sponge rather than drift-ing throughout the house. You can purchase a sanding sponge at most hardware and home center stores.

At this point, the patch is ready for priming.

Patching Larger Holes in Plaster

The process of patching larger holes creates a lot of dust. Wear eye protection and a dust mask, and use drop cloths to catch the dust. You may choose to use a drywall patch or a plaster patch.

Making a Plaster Patch

This project requires a piece of wire lath (sized to the hole being patched), tie wire, needle-nose pliers, tin snips and gypsum plaster. Depending upon the size of the patch, you need a drywall compound tray and knife, or for very large patches, a clean worktable (such a piece of plywood) and a plasterer's hawk.

If you are making a few smaller patches, you can probably mix the plaster in a drywall tray, and apply it with a drywall knife. If you are doing a big job, you need a

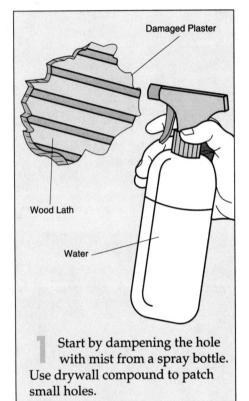

Damaged Plaster

Wood Lath

Water

1 Start by dampening the hole with mist from a spray bottle. Use drywall compound to patch small holes.

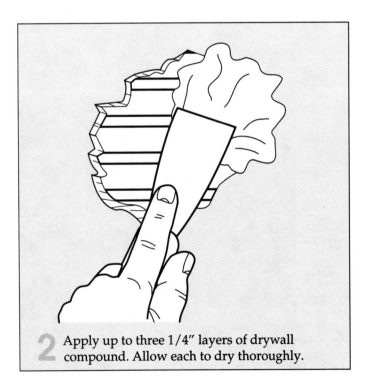

2 Apply up to three 1/4" layers of drywall compound. Allow each to dry thoroughly.

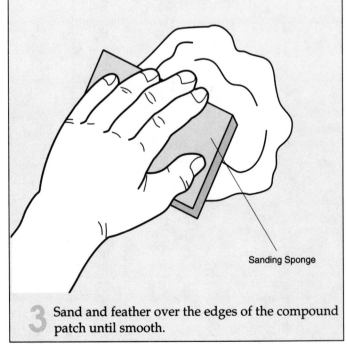

Sanding Sponge

3 Sand and feather over the edges of the compound patch until smooth.

plasterer's hawk and plasterer's trowel. These tools allow you get the plaster on the wall quicker. Plasterer's tools are not common hardware store items, so you may have to go to a quality paint store or plaster supply house to get them.

1 Removing Loose Plaster.
Get rid of any plaster that has lost its hold on the lath, but do not "pick at" sound plaster edges, this only creates a larger hole. To allow for a stronger patch, undercut the old plaster using a can opener. Then, use an old paintbrush or

vacuum to remove chips and dust from the hole.

2 Cutting and Securing Wire Patch. Using tin snips, cut a piece of wire lath slightly smaller than the hole. Rest it on the wood lath. Then stick thin tie wire through the wire lath, looping it behind a piece of the wall's wood lath and then poke it back through the wire lath of the patch. Twist the two ends of the wire together to secure it in place. Do this in as many places as necessary to hold the wire lath flat against the wood lath. Snip the

twisted tie ends short, then bend them flat against the wire lath.

3 Applying the Plaster. If the patch is not too big, mix the plaster in a drywall tray, otherwise mix it in a bucket. Add the appropriate amount of water to the gypsum plaster (read manufacturer's instructions found on the bag). Every grain of plaster must be wet, but you do not want any leftover water. Use a trowel or a 6-inch drywall knife to work the plaster into the lath, applying a coat about 1/4-inch deep. Do not worry about making this layer too smooth. Let the plaster cure thoroughly (most likely overnight). Apply another coat of plaster to bring the patch flush with the intact part of the wall. Let the plaster cure.

4 Applying Drywall Compound.
A final skim coat of drywall compound smooths the rough texture of the plaster and blends the patch into the rest of the wall. Apply the compound with a wide knife or trowel.

5 Feathering the Patch.
With a sanding sponge, feather the edges of the drywall compound, then prime and paint.

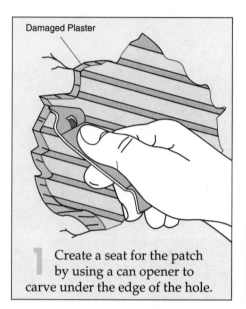

Damaged Plaster

1 Create a seat for the patch by using a can opener to carve under the edge of the hole.

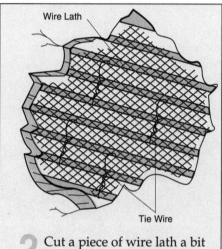

Wire Lath

Tie Wire

2 Cut a piece of wire lath a bit smaller than the hole. Then, secure it using tie wire.

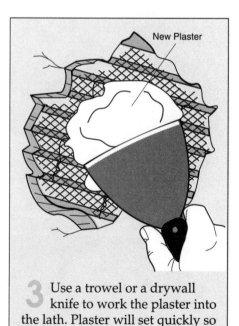

New Plaster

3 Use a trowel or a drywall knife to work the plaster into the lath. Plaster will set quickly so work to get the coat smooth.

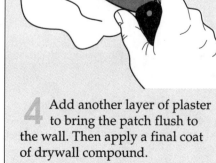

Drywall Compound

4 Add another layer of plaster to bring the patch flush to the wall. Then apply a final coat of drywall compound.

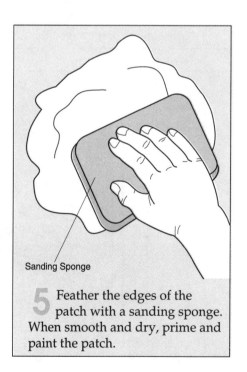

Sanding Sponge

5 Feather the edges of the patch with a sanding sponge. When smooth and dry, prime and paint the patch.

Patching Plaster with Drywall

Plaster walls with large areas of plaster and lath damaged by impact, water exposure, or otherwise flawed, can be repaired with a drywall section. This method replaces the lath behind the damage with 1x4 cleats to support a drywall patch.

1 **Locating the Patch.** Use a drill with a small bit to locate the studs on either side of the damaged plaster. Then drill a rectangular pattern of holes spaced about 1-inch apart along the edges of the damage. Drill the vertical lines of holes right up against the studs as shown. To avoid hitting pipes and wires, pull the drill out when the bit breaks through the lath. Use tape to mark this depth on your bit and always stop drilling at this point. Perforating the plaster in this way will avoid breaking up good plaster around the hole.

2 **Removing damaged area.** Use a drywall saw to cut out the plaster and lath along the rectangular drill holes. Be careful not to sink the saw too deep beyond the lath. Remove any loose plaster around the edges of the cutout.

3 **Installing Cleats.** Measure the hole's length along the studs. Cut 1x4 cleats to fit these measurements. Use drywall screws to secure the vertical cleats along the studs inside the hole. Measure the width between the two cleats. Cut two 1x4 pieces to fit horizontally between cleats. Secure the horizontal pieces by screwing at an angle into the vertical cleats. Use drywall screws, not nails, as more plaster will loosen with hammer blows. Be sure to place the cleats 1/2-inch behind the wall face so the patch will be flush when 1/2-inch drywall is added.

4 **Installing the Patch.** Measure a section of 1/2-inch drywall and secure it to the four cleats using drywall screws. Tape and finish the edges of the patch with drywall tape and compound.

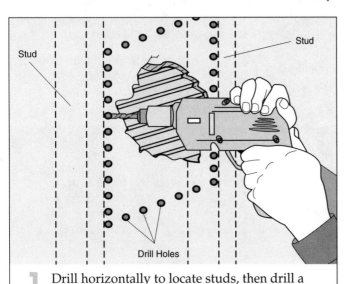

1 Drill horizontally to locate studs, then drill a rectangular pattern inside the studs.

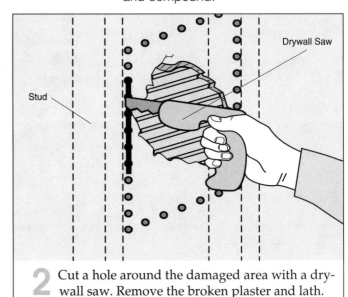

2 Cut a hole around the damaged area with a drywall saw. Remove the broken plaster and lath.

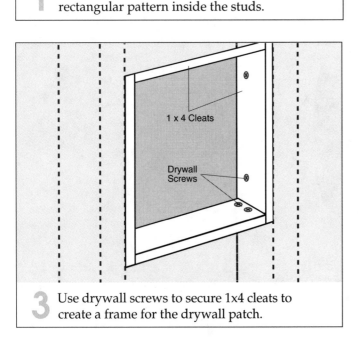

3 Use drywall screws to secure 1x4 cleats to create a frame for the drywall patch.

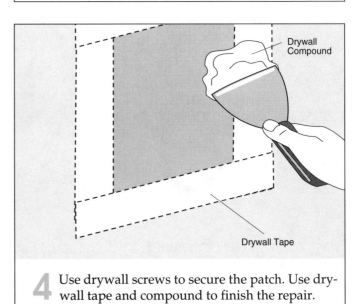

4 Use drywall screws to secure the patch. Use drywall tape and compound to finish the repair.

Patching Larger Holes in Drywall

If you want to repair drywall that is damaged by impact, use the following method.

1 Delineating Damaged Area. Use a framing square to lay out a rectangular repair area. This makes it easy to measure and fit a new piece into the hole.

2 Removing Damaged Area. Drill a hole just inside each of the four corners of the square. Use these holes as starting points for a drywall saw. Saw along the square outline and remove the damaged drywall.

3 Installing Cleats. Cut two pieces of 1x4 at least five inches longer than the vertical size of the hole. Hold the 1x4 against the inside vertical edge of the hole exposing half the width. Then secure the 1x4 with a drywall screw at the top and bottom of the wood. Repeat this procedure with the opposite vertical side. If the patch is larger than about 8 inches, fit horizontal cleats as well. Measure and cut a piece of new wallboard to the size of the hole. Secure with drywall screws driven into the cleats.

4 Finishing the Edges. Bring the edges of the new wallboard patch flush to the wall with tape and drywall compound. When completely cured, sand the drywall compound until smooth.

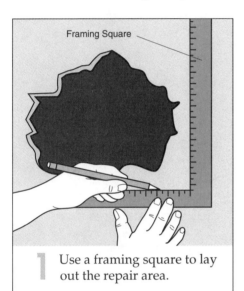

1 Use a framing square to lay out the repair area.

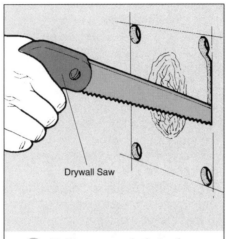

2 Drill a starter hole in the corners of the outline and cut out the damaged piece.

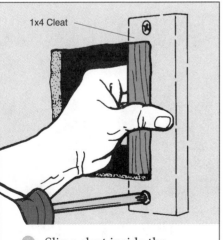

3 Slip a cleat inside the opening and attach with screws through the wallboard.

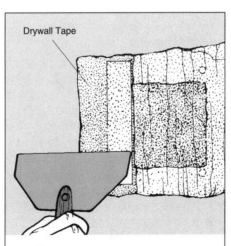

4 Use drywall compound and drywall joint tape to hide the edges of the patch.

Stripping Woodwork with Chemicals

Most woodwork is not worth stripping. Virtually all post-World War II houses, and most twentieth century houses, have woodwork that is paint-grade. This means that it is not highly ornate wood, and was never meant to be coated with a clear finish. Scrape some paint off the woodwork in a few inconspicuous places to determine if it is stain-grade woodwork. Highly-figured oak, cherry, chestnut, or other hardwood, might be worth the time, effort and expense of stripping. However, if you find pine or poplar, it is better simply to patch and sand the woodwork to provide a good surface for painting.

Many paint removers are available. A remover that is cleaned with water is most convenient. In general, thick, paste-type removers containing the active ingredient methylene chloride work better than thin removers that contain solvents such as toluene. Lift the cans of different brands to test their weight—the heaviest is usually the best.

Caution: Virtually all active ingredients used in paint strippers are linked to some ill effects, ranging from skin irritation to cancer. Simply put, nothing that causes paint to bubble is considered harmless. Make sure you are comfortable touching and inhaling any product you choose.

Protecting Yourself

Be very careful when working with paint remover. Work only in a well-ventilated area (preferably outside), and wear heavy rubber gloves and goggles. Paint removers cause nasty chemical burns to skin, and can cause permanent damage to eyes. Keep rags or paper towels available to pick up spatters or spills. Most

Protecting Yourself. For chemical stripping, wear plastic goggles, a half-mask respirator rated for toxic fumes, thick rubber gloves and a long-sleeved shirt.

paint removers are highly flammable (read the label and any cautions). Do not smoke during the job, and do not work near pilot flames (such as gas ranges or water heaters). Do not use power tools on the workpiece.

Chemical paint stripping is warm-weather work. Better results come with higher temperatures because paint removers work by a process of chemical reactions. Paint removers are not good in temperatures below about 75 degrees.

Applying Paint Remover

Use a cheap acrylic-bristle brush (foam brushes melt), brushing in one direction. Apply as much as the workpiece can hold. After about 5 to 10 minutes, remove the paint sludge with a putty knife. If the paint sticks to the workpiece, wait a few minutes and try again. Usually, some paint remains after one application. Repeat the stripping process until all the paint is removed. If some stubborn spots remain, pick them off with a molding scraper, or sand them off. Some woods, particularly oak, retain paint in tiny depressions within the grain, resisting all efforts of removal.

Wipe down the workpiece with clear water, then let it dry thoroughly. At this point, it is ready for sanding and finishing.

Interior woodwork also can be stripped using heat guns or heat plates. These tools, and their use, are discussed in detail in Chapter 2, Exterior Painting. (See page 34-35).

Removing Wallpaper

When it comes to removing wall coverings, you must first determine whether or not the walls were primed (sized) when the covering was hung.

If the walls have been properly primed, and the wall covering is a peelable or strippable vinyl, just peel open a seam and pull it off the wall. Use warm water to wash the paste residue off the walls. After this is done, the walls are ready to be primed.

If you cannot simply peel the wall covering off, then the walls were not primed, and the wall covering may be paper or fabric. You may find multiple layers of wall coverings, and some may have been painted. The covering may peel off easily in some places, while other areas require that you patiently scrape and pick at it piece by piece. Parts of the wall underneath may come off as this is done.

You may already have the tools necessary for removing wall coverings. All you need is a scraper and a spray bottle.

Scrapers. There are two basic types of scrapers. The razor scraper uses replaceable razor blades. It works well on stubborn paper applied to hard plaster, but it has a tendency to gouge soft plaster and drywall. The other type of scraper is like a drywall knife except that it is stiffer and has a beveled edge which enables it to lift the wallpaper off the wall. The beveled blade does not gouge as readily as the razor scraper and removes broader swaths of wallpaper with each stroke. Both tools are available at most paint and wallpaper stores and home centers.

Spray Bottles. An empty glass cleaner bottle works for small jobs, or you can buy a more heavy-duty version at a home center, hardware, or gardening store. A garden spray canister that has a pump and a wand is another effective tool, but in a pinch, you can soak the paper with a big sponge and a bucket of water.

Wallpaper steamers, available at most tool rental houses, may be substituted for the spray bottle, but they do not speed up the job. Steamers are heavy and difficult to work with, and rental fees often are expensive.

Spray Bottles. An empty glass cleaner bottle can be used as a spray bottle, or you can buy a garden spray canister which has a pump and a wand.

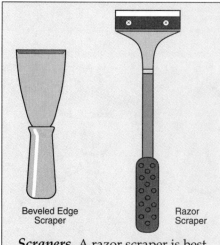

Beveled Edge
Scraper

Razor
Scraper

Scrapers. A razor scraper is best for stubborn paper applied to hard plaster (right). For a softer plaster or drywall, use a scraper that has a beveled edge which lifts the wallpaper off the wall.

1 Removing Dry Wallpaper. Begin removing the dry wallpaper that easily pulls off by hand.

2 Scoring the Paper. Score the wallpaper with the edge of a razor scraper. Do not score too deeply as the lines may show when paint is applied. Water penetrates to the paste through these little cuts.

3 Soaking the Paper. Hot water works alone, or to make the job easier, mix in some wallpaper glue remover (purchased at a hardware store or home center). Do not spray more than you can work with in one hour or so. If you do not scrape an area before it dries, your efforts are wasted. Do go back and spray the same area several times before you start scraping. The more times you spray, the better the liquid penetrates, making it easier for you to remove the wallpaper.

4 Scraping the Paper. Carefully scrape off all layers of wallpaper and any backing. Do not use so much force that you mar the wall surface.

5 Cleaning Paste off the Wall. When all the paper is off, scrub the wall with steel wool dipped in a solution of water and trisodium phosphate. TSP is a strong cleaner available at paint and hardware stores. A final wash with clean, hot water and a sponge leaves the walls smooth and free of paste.

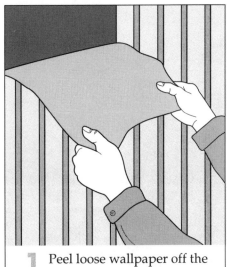

1 Peel loose wallpaper off the wall with your hands.

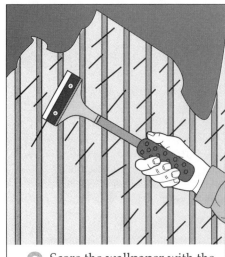

2 Score the wallpaper with the edge of the razor knife.

3 Soak the wallpaper with a spray bottle to loosen its hold on the wall.

4 Carefully scrape off all the wallpaper.

Perforating the Paper

Perforating the paper allows water to soak through to the paste, breaking down the bond. You can buy a tool specifically designed for this purpose. It has sharp, little teeth that roll along the surface. An alternative that also works well is a serrated pizza cutter.

5 Use steel wool to scrub wallpaper paste off the wall.

Final Prep & Sanding

When all wall repairs are made and wall coverings removed, it is time for the final prep and sanding. For best results, wash down walls and woodwork with a household cleaner. This removes any grease or wax that may prevent good adhesion of the paint. Smoke and grease bleed through a new coat of paint so be sure to prime these areas before painting.

As part of the final prep work, set up bright lights to help you work accurately, as well as show defects. Arrange the lights to illuminate the area being worked on, and to eliminate shadows. Halogen work lights are available at most hardware and home center stores, but if you do not want to invest in special lights for painting, bring in a few old lamps (they might get splattered with paint or kicked over). Remove the shades and use 100-watt bulbs.

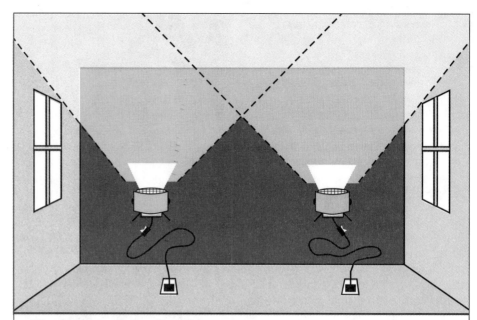

Final Prep and Sanding. Set up bright work lights to show defects and to eliminate shadows.

Wear a Respirator

When sanding drywall compound and plaster patches, wear a respirator that is rated for dust. A half-mask respirator is best, but a disposable mask is acceptable. The respirator must be NIOSH-rated for dust particles as small as 1 micron in diameter.

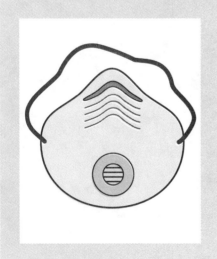

Sanding Block. Sanding walls and ceilings is usually done with hand-held sandpaper or a sanding block. Spend a few dollars on a sanding block, or make one by wrapping sandpaper around a scrap piece of 2x4. A sanding block saves some effort and wear and tear on your hands. It also helps make surfaces flatter, since a piece of hand-held sandpaper will conform to surface irregularities. But for tight corners or other hard-to-reach areas, there is no substitute for folding the sandpaper into a rectangle, and sanding by hand.

Sanding Pole. For a big sanding job, a pole sander which consists of a stick with a metal-backed foam pad, is indispensable. The pad is equipped with clamps that hold a half-sheet of sandpaper. It is attached to the pole with a universal joint that allows the pole to be held at any angle. A pole sander is good for sanding in long strokes, and producing a uniform surface. It also helps you reach ceilings without climbing a ladder. Pole sanders are available at drywall supply houses, paint stores and home center stores.

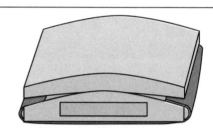

Sanding Block. A sanding block is great for sanding patches.

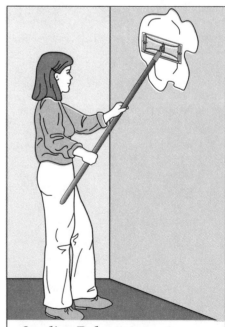

Sanding Pole. Pole sanders are helpful for big jobs and hard-to-reach areas.

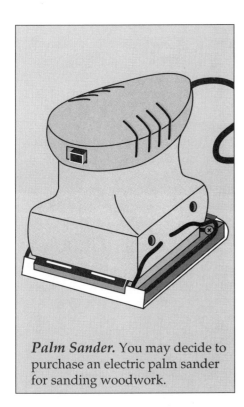

Palm Sander. You may decide to purchase an electric palm sander for sanding woodwork.

Palm Sander. A small vibrating palm sander is great for sanding woodwork. On all but the smallest jobs, the cost of a vibrating sander is money well spent. A sander lasts for years, and is useful for all kinds of refinishing jobs.

Sanding the Interior

Almost all interior sanding is done with either 60-grit or 100-grit sandpaper. The 60-grit paper takes care of runs and drips, and built-up paint on the edges of doors and windows. For most sanding, such as feathering drywall compound and removing gloss from surfaces before repainting, 100-grit paper does the job.

Change sandpaper sheets frequently. Working with clogged sandpaper is a waste of time and effort. For a big job, buy sandpaper in bulk (a pack of 100 sheets); buying a few sheets at a time can get expensive.

When sanding, use your free hand to check the area for smoothness. The rule is simple: Bumps and ridges you can feel with your

hand will appear when the surface is painted.

Going over it All

When you think you are finished sanding, take a break. The break allows you to "forget" the hundreds of little decisions you made about what is just right, and what is good enough.

Return to the job with a bright lamp and hold it near the wall so that the light rakes against the surface, highlighting imperfections. Do any necessary touch-up.

Cleaning Up

Sanding drywall compound and old paint produces a lot of fine dust which settles on the tops of window and door surrounds, and on baseboards and walls. It must be carefully cleaned up before the paint job begins. Vacuum all surfaces, and wipe them down with a damp cloth. If there is a lot of dust on the drop cloths, take them outside to shake them before putting them back in place.

Going Over it All. Shine a raking light against the wall to reveal any defects. Sand any imperfections.

Testing for Lead in Paint

Test kits that detect lead content in paint are available at many hardware stores. If your house was built before 1970, it is best to assume the presence of lead paint. Sanding lead paint produces lead-laced dust, a cause of lead poisoning which results in aches, pains and fatigue, and in extreme cases, brain damage. Children are most at risk from lead poisoning, so they must stay out of areas where lead dust might be present. Pregnant women (or women who may be pregnant) must also stay out of these areas, because blood-borne lead can harm a developing fetus.

Carefully seal off the work area with polyethylene sheeting secured with duct tape around door openings. Wear a respirator when sanding paint that might contain lead. Do not smoke while in the work area (smoking promotes lead inhalation and ingestion), and vigorously wash your hands before eating or drinking. Clean up the work area thoroughly (vacuum and damp-mop), and wash work clothes at the end of each work day.

It is a good idea to have children tested for lead periodically. The blood test is simple and inexpensive, and can be done by a pediatrician or family doctor.

Masking Hardware & Edges

Some hardware, such as door lock sets (the part that sticks out the edge of the door) and hinges, are masked before painting starts. If you are painting just the walls, trim edges such as window and door surrounds and baseboards, also must be masked.

Using Masking Tape

It is best to use painter's masking tape rather than other types because it has a lighter adhesive. Trimming tape edges with a craft knife is easier and neater than trying to apply the tape in perfectly straight lines. Painter's masking tape is available at paint stores.

Using a Paint Guide

A paint guide helps get paint into tight corners, while keeping it off ceilings or trim. Be careful not to get paint on the back of the paint guide. It is disappointing when a "neatness" tool ends up making a mess. Paint guides are available at paint stores.

Priming

Primer is used to seal in stains and to provide a consistent, slightly grainy surface that enhances the bond between the finish paint and the painted surface. It is also the final, and often most critical, step of interior preparation. All bare wood and stained woodwork is primed before the finish paint goes on. Water-stained areas, and those areas that once had wallpaper on them also must be primed.

An added benefit of priming is that it highlights imperfections that otherwise might be missed, providing a last chance to repair minor defects such as ridges in patches, poorly-feathered edges, or nicks and scrapes.

Bare wood is primed to keep finish paint from soaking into the wood

Using Masking Tape. Mask all hardware before beginning to paint.

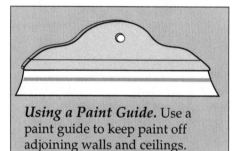

Using a Paint Guide. Use a paint guide to keep paint off adjoining walls and ceilings.

and to provide a consistently toothy surface for the finish paint. Do not skip this step. Painted wood that is not primed looks dull and the knots in the wood inevitably bleed through.

Stained surfaces (even those that are varnished) must be primed before painting, otherwise the stain bleeds through the new top coat of paint. Water stains, such as those on leak-stained ceilings, also bleed through finish paint if left unprimed.

Other imperfections, such as crayon marks, marker stains, food stains, or areas where adhesive tape once stuck, must be primed as well.

Choosing a Primer

For most priming jobs, any good-quality interior primer is sufficient. Primers are available in water-based and oil-based formulas.

Some stubborn stains, such as dark-colored wood stains or large yellowish water stains, even bleed

through the primer. For these stains, shellac or shellac-based primers may be the only solution. Shellac is alcohol-based, highly flammable and the fumes are intense and persistent. If you have to use a shellac-based primer, apply it with a throwaway brush or roller. Shellac dries within minutes, making brush cleanup almost impossible. Continue applying coats of primer over the shellac coat until stains no longer bleed through.

Painting the Right Way

The devil, they say, is in the details. There is a right way to hold a brush, a right way to maneuver a roller, a right to spray, and a right place to start and stop for the day.

There are purists who insist that anything less than a fully brush-painted job does not look quite right. However, most painters "cut in" with

Using a Bucket

Most painters find it easier to work with a partially-filled paint bucket than to work straight from the paint can. Pour an inch or two of paint into the bottom of an empty bucket. This way you have:

■ A place to rest the brush, allowing you to work with two hands if necessary;

■ Fewer spatters;

■ Less to clean if you tip over the bucket.

a brush, then finish off walls and ceilings with a roller. Brushing is best for wood trim, and spraying is generally not the best option for interior jobs.

Using a Pothook. When working on a ladder, use a good-quality pothook to hold the bucket. Good pothooks are inexpensive and available at virtually all paint and hardware stores. Do not rig up a mock pothook with wire or a coat hanger.

Having a Rag Ready. Before you start painting, put a dust rag or dust brush in your pocket. This allows you to knock down spider webs or to dust the top of a door or window surround as you work around the room.

Getting a Better Grip. Many people instinctively grab a paintbrush with a handshake grip. A better grip is more like a pencil grip, with the fingers and thumb wrapped around the metal ferrule. This grip allows the hand and wrist a full range of motion, providing greater speed and precision. If your hand cramps, switch hands or switch temporarily to the handshake grip.

Choosing a Brush. As a general rule, use the largest brush you are comfortable with. Professional painters seldom pick up anything

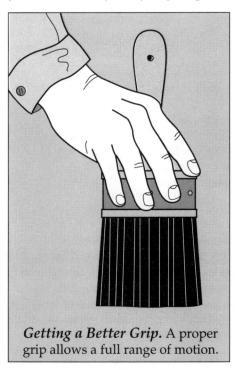

Getting a Better Grip. A proper grip allows a full range of motion.

smaller than a 4-inch brush. Most homeowners achieve the best results with a 4-inch brush for cutting in and large surfaces, and an angled 2½-inch to 3-inch sash brush for details such as windows and doors.

Use the correct brush for the paint being used. Oil-based paints require a natural bristle, called "China bristles", while water-based paints are applied with a synthetic bristle brush.

Brushing Techniques

For a clean, even surface there is a right way and a wrong way to apply paint. With a little practice, you will master the technique.

1 Laying on the Paint. Dip the brush about 1 inch into the paint. As you remove the brush from the bucket, slap the brush lightly against the side to remove excess paint. Do not overdo it—you do not want the brush to be dry when it comes out of the can. The more paint on the brush, the faster the work. A properly loaded brush drips when pulled out of the can bristles-down. To prevent excessive dripping, gently swing the brush up to a horizontal position as it leaves the can, and move the brush quickly to the surface to be painted.

Pulling the brush out of the bucket and across the work surface lays on the paint. The laying-on strokes do not have to be neat. Simply wipe the paint onto the work surface in two strokes—one from one side of the brush, one from the other.

2 Brushing out the Paint. Brush out the paint using long, even, parallel strokes. Use enough pressure to bend the bristles just a little.

3 Tipping off the Paint. Finish off the leading edge of the paint by tipping off; that is, gradually pulling the bristles off the surface. Think of an airplane leaving the runway. As you paint, keep a wet edge. This means painting from a dry area slightly into the previously painted, still-wet area. Feather edges by tipping off.

1 Just lay the paint on the surface, it does not have to be neat.

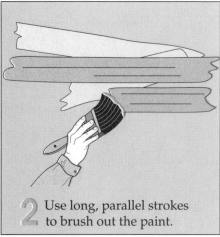

2 Use long, parallel strokes to brush out the paint.

3 The leading edge of the paint is finished by a technique called "tipping off." That is, gradually pulling the bristles of the brush off the painted surface.

Painting a Straight Line.

To paint a straight line, such as a wall-to-trim joint, clean one edge of the brush on the side of the paint bucket. This leaves one edge of the brush nearly dry. With the wet side of the brush along the line, pull the brush on edge with the bristles slightly bent (just enough to bring all of the bristles into contact with the surface).

Using the brush on edge tends to streak the paint slightly. When the straight line is finished, even out the paint by going over it with the brush on the broad side.

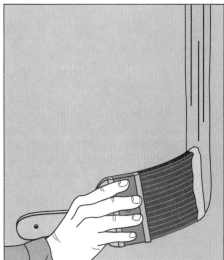

Painting a Straight Line. Hold the brush like a pencil, painting with the edge of the bristles.

Painting Order

There are no rules that say a certain part of the room must be painted first, but in general, rooms are painted from the top down. Begin with the ceiling. If you are priming new drywall, move right from priming the ceiling to priming the woodwork. If you are painting the walls a different color than the ceiling, put one coat on the ceiling, let it dry, then paint the walls. If you are adding another coat, repeat the sequence. If the woodwork is a different color than the walls, it is easiest to paint the walls, let them dry, then paint the woodwork. Repeat the sequence for a second coat.

Rolling Technique

Rollers are much faster than brushes for painting walls and ceilings. Virtually all painters choose to paint walls and ceilings with a roller. The only disadvantage to using a roller is roller spray. As the paint is rolled, droplets fly into the air. The thinner the paint and the faster the roller moves, the more roller spray results. Even within a product line, some paints spray more than others. With a little practice, you will learn how to keep the spray manageable.

Rollers leave a slightly dimpled finish on the painted surface. Only a skillful painter using a brush achieves a glassy-smooth surface. However, rollers have been in common use for 50 years and it is extremely rare to find a painter who brushes walls and ceilings. Today, roller-painted surfaces are the accepted standard.

A brushed finish is still the standard for woodwork, such as doors, windows, trim and cabinet work. As long as you brush along the grain of the wood, the brush strokes will blend. Resist the urge to speed up trim painting by using a roller. Even the smoothest roller leaves a slightly stippled finish.

At this point this book focuses on the use of latex paint only, (since latex is highly recommended for rolling and interior work in general) and the use of two colors (one for the ceiling and one for the walls).

If the room is completely cut-in and allowed to dry before the rolling begins, a visible line shows up where the cut-in meets the rolled area. The effect is very slight, virtually unnoticeable if you are using a high-quality flat paint. Even with a semi-gloss paint this line bothers only the most extreme perfectionists. By using a helper to keep a wet edge, you can make the line disappear. As you cut in four of five feet along the ceiling, have your helper roll this area, working along with you

Tips for Painting

■ A new paint job appears splotchy while it is drying. This is normal. Avoid the urge to return to just-painted areas in an attempt to even out the finish. If you are doing a reasonably good job, the finish will look even when it is dry.

■ On wood surfaces, such as doors or windows, brush in the direction of the wood grain. All brushing leaves brush strokes, but they are less noticeable when they run in the direction of the wood grain.

■ Paint will inevitably run down the bristles of the brush toward the ferrule. To keep it from running over the ferrule, clear the brush from time to time by running both sides along the lip of the can; or by applying the built-up paint in the brush to the work surface, then brushing the paint out. If paint starts to run over the ferrule, stop painting at the next logical break and clean the brush.

■ Check for drips or sags every 10 to 15 minutes as you work.

If the paint is still wet, brush out drips or sags. If the paint is tacky, let drips and sags dry completely, then sand out the imperfections and touch up.

■ If you have to stop before the paint job is done, stop at a logical break point, such as a corner or the end of a piece of trim. Carry the paint all the way to the break point. Do not worry about getting it on the adjoining unpainted surface—it is better to overrun the break point than to stop short of it.

all the way around the room. Please note: Keeping a wet edge at the cut-in line is a must when working with oil-based paint because the line is more pronounced.

If working alone, you can keep a wet edge by switching from brush to roller frequently.

Rolling a Ceiling

Rolling a ceiling is no more difficult than rolling the walls. One thing you must be careful about, however is where you place the paint can; you don't want to knock it over as you study the ceiling above.

1 Cutting in the Ceiling. Use a two- or three-inch brush to cut in around the edge of the ceiling. If some paint gets on the wall surfaces, wipe it off with a rag. Cut in around light fixtures and ceiling fans.

2 Checking the Roller. Place the roller cover on the frame, making sure that the end of the cover is flush with the end of the frame. Make sure the nap is clean and none of the fibers are coming off.

Ceiling work is faster if the roller is mounted on an extension pole. In this case, place the roller tray on the floor Some people prefer to work from a ladder to gain the close-up control of holding the roller handle. In this case, use the hooks on the bottom of the paint tray to secure the tray to the ladder's shelf.

3 Loading the Paint Tray. Fill the bottom portion of the tray with paint. Try to keep the paint off the can label as it is poured; you may need to read the label directions or specifications later. Inexpensive guards (they look like the bill of a cap) keep paint off the label and out of the top of the can.

Use a brush to clean up the top of the can, then set the cover loosely on top. Put the can in an out-of-the-way place, preferably just outside the room so you do not have to worry about kicking it over as you work.

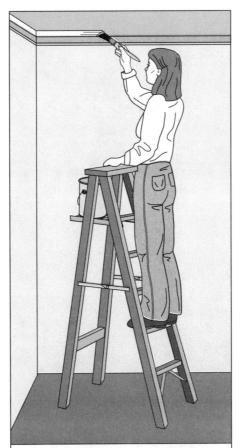

1 Use a 2" or 3" brush to cut in the ceiling. Wipe off any paint that gets on the wall surface.

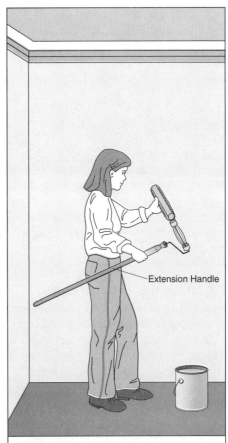

Extension Handle

2 Place the roller cover on the frame. An extension handle is especially helpful for painting ceilings.

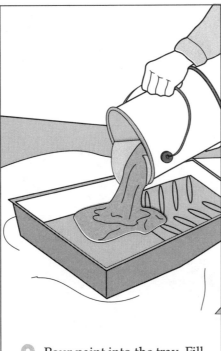

3 Pour paint into the tray. Fill the bottom part of the tray.

Helpful Hint

To keep things neat punch a few nail holes through the rim of the can to allow the paint to run back down rather than accumulating along the rim.

4 Loading the Roller. Dip the roller into the paint. Use the sloped part of the tray to roll off the excess. Repeat the process until the roller is saturated, but not dripping.

5 Laying on the Paint. Apply paint in a zigzag "N" or "W" pattern. The idea is not to paint neat zigzags (which is hard to do with an extension pole anyway). The idea is to roughly apply the paint, which is spread out evenly in subsequent strokes. Lay the zigzag pattern over an area that is within comfortable reach (typically about three feet by five feet).

6 Rolling out the Paint. Roll using even strokes that overlap the edges at the beginning and end. Continue painting in sections, overlapping from each "new" area into the just-painted area, thus keeping a wet edge. As you come to the end of a stroke do not simply stop rolling and then lift the roller. Instead keep rolling as you lift, like a plane leaving the runway.

Watch for roller marks as you apply the paint. Roller marks are thin lines caused by a buildup of paint that flows off the edges of the roller. They also are caused by putting excess pressure on the roller. If lines appear, try using less pressure. If the paint is not adhering properly it is probably not because you are pushing too softly. Most likely it is because the roller needs more paint. Do not make the mistake so many beginners make by "dry rolling." Keep the roller loaded with paint for an even coat.

Check frequently for runs or drips. If you see imperfections in a wet area, eliminate them by going over the area with a fairly dry roller. Be careful though, not to re-roll areas that have started to become tacky. Doing this causes an "orange-peel" effect that may not blend in when the paint dries. If you create an objectionable orange-peeled area, sand it out and repaint the entire surface.

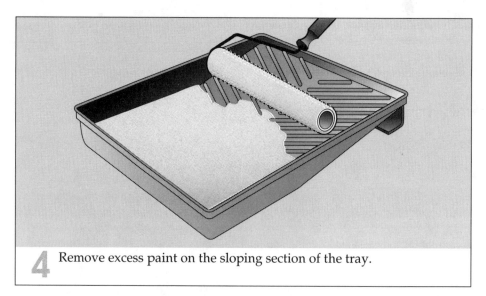

4 Remove excess paint on the sloping section of the tray.

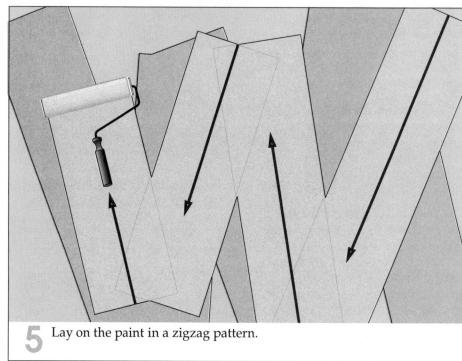

5 Lay on the paint in a zigzag pattern.

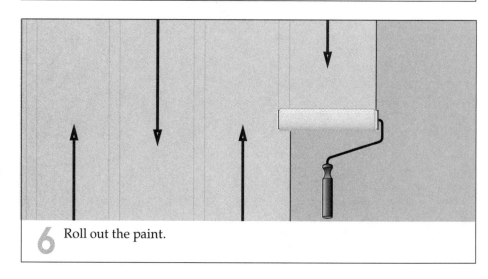

6 Roll out the paint.

Rolling the Walls

Virtually all jobs require two coats of paint. One exception is a job that requires a color that closely matches the new color. The second coat is applied the same way as the first coat. Avoid the temptation to skip the cutting-in process. Once the paint is dry, this short-cut becomes obvious.

Let each ceiling coat dry completely before moving onto a wall coat. Cut-in the wall-to-ceiling joint, being careful to draw a straight line at the freshly-painted ceiling. (Mistakes are touched up at the end of the job.) Cut-in around doors and windows, in tight areas (less than a roller width) between trim and wall joints, in the corners, and at all wall-to-baseboard joints.

Painting Door & Window Casing

The first decision when painting windows and doors is whether to wrap or face off the casing. Most modern, post-World War II trim is comprised of flat boards which can be handled either way. In general though, wrapping looks best on thicker moldings. Many older houses have trim with rounded edges that do not provide the sharp edge necessary for facing off. Therefore they must be wrapped.

Either way, start at the outside edge of the trim and keep a wet edge as you paint.

Wrapping. Take the trim color around the side of the trim boards so that the trim color meets the wall color at the wall. Wrapping requires that you draw sharp lines where the trim meets the wall. This is slow and tedious work.

Facing off. Bring the wall color onto the outside edges of the trim, and start the trim color on the face of the trim. Wipe off any wall paint that accidentally brushes onto the face of the trim. If the paint is not wiped off as you go, the result is a visible, fat edge.

Painting Doors

There are two big reasons to paint doors carefully: First, since door panels are large, flat surfaces located at eyeball level, doors get noticed. Secondly, doors are functional moving parts, so you want to avoid building up fat edges of paint which prevent doors from closing properly.

Doors are carefully prepared, to remove old paint drips and fat edges, and to ensure a good bond between the old paint and new paint. A good "prep" job requires sanding. Use an electric palm sander for the quickest results. If you do not have a palm sander, sand the door by hand. If old runs and drips require coarse sandpaper, start with 60-grit paper and finish up with 100-grit paper. You may need to do a little work with a pull scraper to get the door in good functioning order.

For best results, prime doors with a good-quality primer. If the doors are flat, prime the edges with a brush and then use a roller to prime the faces. Do the same when you apply paint.

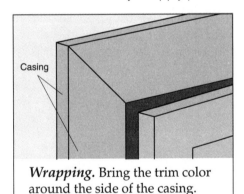

Wrapping. Bring the trim color around the side of the casing.

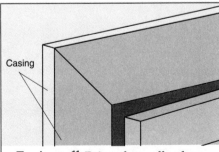

Facing off. Bring the wall color to the outside edges of the casing. Start the trim color on the face of the casing.

If the door has raised panels, it should be primed and painted.

1 **Painting Edges.** As you paint the edges, use a rag to wipe off paint that accumulates on the front and back of the door.

2 **Painting Panels.** Paint the door panels next, working from the top down.

1 Paint the door edges first.

2 Paint the door panels working from the top down.

3 **Painting Rails.** The rails are the horizontal members at the top, middle and bottom on a two or four-panel door. Brush out the paint with final strokes that run the full width of the door.

3 Paint the rails.

4 Paint the stiles.

4 **Painting Stiles.** The stiles are the vertical members on both sides of the panels. Again, work from top to bottom and finish with long, continuous brush strokes. Look for drips, sags and runs as you work. Paint often runs off the corners of the panels. Brush out any imperfections and drips on the door, but do not run a brush repeatedly over tacky paint. This results in noticeable shiny spots called flashing (see page 61).

Painting Windows

There are three common types of windows: double-hung, casement and fixed sash. Double-hung windows are the most common; they are the familiar guillotine-type window, with sliding top and bottom sash. Casement windows open like doors; some are controlled by cranks, others are controlled by push rods or handles. Fixed sash windows are those that do not open.

Keeping Paint off Window Parts. Rule one for painting windows: Do not get paint in the window works. Usually this simply means keeping paint out of the window channels. It does not matter if you are painting the windows white and the channels are dark-stained wood. Resist the urge for uniformity. If you paint the channels, the sash will stick and the windows will not work properly. Either live with the contrast in colors, or put up some curtains.

If you are painting older windows that have sash weight cords or chains, do not paint the cords, chains or pulleys. If you get paint on these parts, there is a good chance that the windows will not work properly.

With casement windows, be sure to keep paint out of the cranks, push rods, handles and hinges.

Freeing a Stuck Window. If you find that a window sash was painted shut during the last paint job, free it by using a putty knife or utility knife to cut the paint film binding the sash to

the window frame. The window may be painted shut on the inside or outside. Do not bang on the window sash with a hammer. If a window needs a little "persuading," place a wood block against the sash and tap gently. Be careful not to knock sash corners apart.

Freeing a Stuck Window. Cut the paint film that binds the sash to the frame. You may have to do this on both sides of the window.

Double-Hung Windows

If you have not already removed the sash lock hardware, do it now. Place the hardware in plastic bags so small parts and screws do not get lost. Apply only one coat of paint to meeting edges, such as sash rails and sash-to-frame joints. A paint buildup at these joints can prevent the window from opening and closing easily.

When you paint the window sash, it is nearly impossible to keep paint off the glass. Fortunately, dried paint comes off glass very easily so, when painting the sash, let the paint lap onto the glass about 1/4 inch. After the paint dries, remove the overlap as described in Step 4.

1 Beginning the Upper Sash.
Pull the upper sash down at least an inch to make it easier to paint the top rail. Check the top edge of each sash for any paint build-up. Sand or scrape off fat edges (if any). Paint build-up on the top of either sash can prevent the window from closing properly.

2 Finishing Upper Sash. Push the lower sash all the way up. Then pull the upper sash down to expose the unpainted bottom portion. Finish painting the upper sash. Push the upper sash up to within about an inch of closing to let the top rail dry before pushing it into its channel.

3 Painting Lower Sash. Pull the lower sash down to a comfortable level for painting. Do not push it into the bottom channel. This allows you to paint the entire bottom rail. Then, paint the lower sash working from top to bottom.

4 Removing Paint from Glass. Use a straightedge to score a line along the glass where the paint will end. Then use a window scraper to remove the paint. This tool is designed to hold a single-edged razor blade. With a sharp blade the paint easily peels off in long ribbons.

Casement Windows

Casement windows are painted in this order: hinge edge, muntins, then top, bottom, and sides of sash, and finally the frame. Remember to sand out fat edges before painting. Keep paint out of hinges. When the paint becomes tacky, rotate the sash in and out slightly to break the paint film.

1 Pull down the upper sash of a double-hung window and paint the top of that sash.

2 Push the lower sash all the way up and finish the rest of the upper sash.

3 Push up the upper sash, leaving a 1" gap at the top. Pull lower sash down and paint.

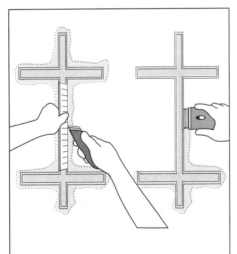

4 Use a window scraper to remove excess paint from windows.

Flashing

Flashing is a shiny spotting effect that occurs when wet paint is applied over an area of dry paint. The painted area may flash even if you use the same paint, from the same can, applied with the same brush within a half-hour. High-gloss paints are more prone to flashing than semi-gloss or flat paints, and some colors tend to flash more than others. Keeping a wet edge helps prevent flashing.

Flashing is not much of a consideration for most interior painting jobs that use low-gloss latex paint. However, if semi-gloss or gloss paint is used, you must be scrupulously careful about keeping a wet edge.

Flashing is particularly obvious on touch-ups on enamel-painted wood trim, such as doors and window frames.

If the paint flashes, there is no way to fix it. Either live with the results, or do the job over carefully keeping a wet edge.

Pausing & Stopping

If you must pause or stop in the middle of the job, do not simply drop everything and run. There are a few things that need to be done first.

Pausing a Brush Job

If you need to pause a brush job, for an hour or two, wrap the brush in plastic wrap and place it out of sunlight. The plastic wrap keeps the paint from drying out. Close the paint can and place it out of sunlight as well.

To put the job on hold overnight, wrap the brush thoroughly in plastic wrap, and store it in the refrigerator. Cooling the brush delays evaporation for several hours. A brush can be stored overnight or longer by soaking it in water or turpentine, depending on the base of the paint being used.

Pausing a Roller Job

To pause for an hour or two, dip the roller to thoroughly load it, but do not roll out the excess. Cover the tray with a piece of plastic wrap.

To stop overnight, double-wrap the fully-loaded roller in plastic wrap and store it in the refrigerator.

You can clean nylon roller covers, but it takes a long time to wash all the paint out of them and most people consider them cheap enough to discard at the end of the job. A good lamb's wool roller is worth the effort of a thorough washing (use warm water and dish washing liquid). Store the roller on end, so it does not develop a flat spot. Clean the roller frame and paint tray outside if possible. If necessary, finish cleaning over a sink, using warm water and dish washing liquid. Rinse out the sink drain thoroughly.

If you are rolling oil-based paint, it is never worth cleaning a nylon roller cover. Clean a good-quality lamb's wool roller by soaking it thoroughly in turpentine and mineral spirits three times.

Cleaning Up

Even when the paint job is finished, there is a lot of work left to be done. Besides cleaning off yourself, you will want to clean all of your tools so they remain in good condition.

Latex. Use dish washing liquid and plenty of running water to remove latex from yourself and your painting tools. Squeeze the brush frequently and use a wire brush to get paint out of the area around the ferrule. If you are working in a sink or bathtub, let the water run for a few minutes after you have cleaned everything to make sure the paint clears out of the drain. Gummed up paint clogs plumbing.

Shake the brush out, then slap it across a clean, dry surface to remove the last of the water. Place the brush back in its protective jacket (or a piece of butcher paper) and hang it on a hook.

Oil-Base. Wear rubber gloves to protect your hands. Wash the brush repeatedly in an inch or two of mineral spirits, squeezing and massaging the brush frequently to remove built-up paint. Clean the ferrule area gently with a wire brush. When you think the brush is clean (mineral spirits coming out of the brush run clear), do one final rinse in a clean container of mineral spirits. Shake and slap the brush dry, then store it in a protective jacket or butcher paper. (See pages 74-75).

Removing Drips

After the painting is done and the drop cloths are removed, you may find a paint drip or two.

If it is oil-based paint, let it dry thoroughly, then try to pop it off the surface with a razor blade. If the drip is on carpet, "shave" it off with a razor blade.

If the drip is latex paint scrub it with a damp cloth. If that does not work, wipe it up with a commercial paint remover.

Discarding the Leftovers

What to do with leftover paints and solvents, such as mineral spirits and paint thinner, is an environmental issue that has yet to be resolved. Many waste disposal contractors will not knowingly pick up or discard paint, paint cans or solvents. To determine the rules and requirements in your town, call the local waste disposal agency (or contractor). Local practices vary. In some places, it is still legal to toss the leftover paint into the garbage and let the trash hauler deal with it.

Some municipalities require contractors and homeowners to take discarded paint to special pickup points, or to treat paint and solvents as toxic waste.

Other local agencies take a middle-of-the-road approach, and encourage citizens to open containers of leftover paint and solvent, let the liquid evaporate, then discard the containers.

DECORATIVE PAINT FINISHES

Take your interior painting skills one step further with the techniques described in this chapter. These techniques are surprisingly simple to learn. Yet you can use them to create faux finishes that will turn an ordinary room into a unique place that expresses your own creativity.

Personalizing Your Painting

There are certain rooms that are distinctive because of an interesting shape; or because they are decorated with unique furniture; or command an impressive view. In these rooms the painting should be inconspicuous to highlight special elements. Other rooms lack stand-out features and are uninteresting living spaces. These rooms will be transformed with decorative paint finishes and become highlights of your home.

Decorative painting is easier than you might think. In most cases, you'll do the same preparation work and base coat as you would for any interior paint job. Then you will apply one or more coats of semi-transparent glazes that produce compelling textures and color schemes. Choose glaze colors that complement or contrast with the base color. The colors you choose, the opacity of the glaze, the number of paint and glaze layers, and the way you manipulate the glaze coat all combine to create different effects. Test your method on paper before beginning an actual project. This will give you a chance to perfect your technique and to make sure you like the way the colors look once they have dried.

Decorative paint finishes are not only for walls. Some designs are suited to large, unbroken surfaces but other designs are more intricate and look good on smaller objects. Kitchen and bath cabinets, clothing chests, coffee tables, and desks are just some of the objects than can be enhanced with decorative painting.

The Tools of Decorative Painting

For a decorative finish to look good, you must start with a well-prepared surface and a good even base coat of solid color. You'll need the techniques described in Chapter Three, "Interior Painting". Floors must be covered with drop clothes. Walls must be smooth: all cracks and holes filled and sanded. Apply a solid base coat with high quality brushes and rollers. Each of the specific techniques described here will tell you which kind of paint to use for the finish.

Specialty Tools

These tools are necessary to create the various decorative paint finishes. Read the section about a technique first, the process may not require all these materials.

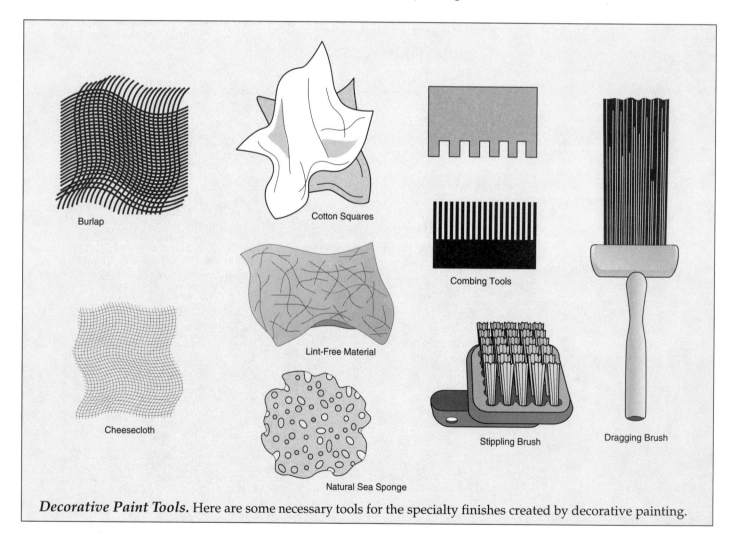

Burlap

Cheesecloth

Cotton Squares

Lint-Free Material

Natural Sea Sponge

Combing Tools

Stippling Brush

Dragging Brush

Decorative Paint Tools. Here are some necessary tools for the specialty finishes created by decorative painting.

Natural Sea Sponge. These sponges are available at art stores. They have the texture and irregular shape you'll need for the sponging technique. They can be cleaned and used numerous times. If you are unable to buy a natural sponge, you can use a large synthetic sponge if you rip off all the hard edges and corners.

Lint-Free Rags or Cheesecloth. For the ragging and rag rolling techniques use clean cotton rags or cheesecloth with no loose ends.

Stippling Brush. A stippling brush is a large, square brush with short, very fine bristles. They can be expensive but are worth the price for the finish they make on large surfaces. For smaller surfaces a shoe brush, clothes brush or short stain brush will do the job. Available at art supply and paint stores.

Dragging Brush. This technique requires a brush with long clusters of bristles called a dragging brush, over-grainer, or flogger brush. These brushes can be purchased at art supply stores or through mail-order catalogs. Keep this tool dry and fairly clean while dragging or it will not pick up glaze.

Combing Tool. The combing technique can employ a great variety of comb-like tools. Combs are available from art stores or mail-order catalogs. They come in metal, plastic, wood or rubber and have varying teeth width and length. You can create a tooth pattern from heavy stock cardboard or from a plastic lid cut in half. Use a material that will not bend under the pressure of dragging. Don't make the spaces too narrow or glaze will fill in them and not create a pattern.

Water and Oil-based Glazes

The glaze used as the transparent color layer is similar to regular paint except that it has much less pigment. Like paint, glaze comes as oil-based or as water-based latex. Use oil-based glaze over oil paint or latex paint. Water-based glaze can only be used on latex paint.

Both oil and water-based glaze can be bought at home center paint departments, hardware stores, paint stores and art supply stores. Water-based glaze is an opaque, gel-like acrylic medium that is mixed with water. It gets it's color by adding artist's acrylic colors, universal tints or thinned latex paint.

Oil-based glazes get color from artist's oil paints, universal tints or oil-based paint diluted with thinner. You can make your own oil glaze by mixing three parts turpentine with one part boiled linseed oil and then adding a few drops of paint drier or similar resin. Mix in your own artist's oils, universal tints or thinned oil-based paint. Experiment with colors in small cups before mixing large quantities. The color is concentrated, so add just a few drops at a time. Just be sure to remember the ratios used when you find a color you like.

Surface Preparation

It is very important to prepare surfaces correctly before any painting project. Paint will not bond correctly and surface flaws will be highlighted if inadequately prepared. Decorative finishes usually have a gloss that will emphasize cracks and holes.

When you are preparing walls, remove any loose plaster or drywall. Remove wallpaper and scrub the walls clean of wallpaper paste. Fill all cracks and holes with patching compound. Allow the compound to dry, then sand it smooth. For further information on surface preparation see page 45-53.

When preparing wood surfaces such as cabinets, furniture or trim, remove any loose paint. Sand or chemically de-gloss varnished surfaces.

Surfaces need to be non-porous for the glaze to stand out, therefore priming is an essential step. Make sure the surface is smooth and dirt-free before priming. If you are priming bare wood or walls that were papered, use alkyd primer. You can use latex primer on walls that have never been papered, are in good condition, and will be painted and glazed with latex.

Applying the Base Coat

When the surface is prepared and primed you are ready to apply the base coat. Remember that the over all effect depends on this color so you

Applying the Base Coat. An evenly applied base coat over a well prepared surface is necessary for effective decorative painting.

must apply it to the surface evenly and without brush or roller marks. Use long, overlapping parallel strokes of the roller or brush. If you are brushing woodwork, be sure to stroke with the grain. Brush marks are more evident in higher gloss paints so use high quality brushes which create softer lines. Be sure to allow adequate drying time between all layers of paint. Paint may feel dry on top but could be wet beneath the skin and will bleed through when you begin dabbing the surface.

Glazing Techniques

All of the following techniques are applied on a surface that is properly prepared, primed if necessary, and thoroughly base coated. Decorative paint techniques all employ the same formula of a gloss, eggshell, or satin base color that is seen through the broken color and translucence of one or more top coats of colored glaze. The differences lie in whether the glaze is added or subtracted on the surface and how it is moved about. Results are quite pleasing with simple rags moved skillfully, but can be even more striking by using special brushes and tools. One of the keys to decorative finishes is to have a consistent flow, even in broken color effects. Keep your hand moving. Don't go back over an area until the project is dry, and then add color sparingly.

Sponging

Use the sponging technique for walls, ceilings, flat surfaced furniture and cabinets. Sponging creates an illusion of depth by having multiple layers of broken color over a base color. This is perhaps the easiest of all the techniques as the goal is a random, uneven pattern. Don't over-sponge or you'll get muddled and splotchy areas instead of the fields of dotted color you are after. It's best to use a natural, sea sponge because of the irregular shape but a synthetic sponge can be torn to remove all flat surfaces and edges.

1 Mix the paint into the glaze. Stir together well and add color slowly to achieve the shade desired.

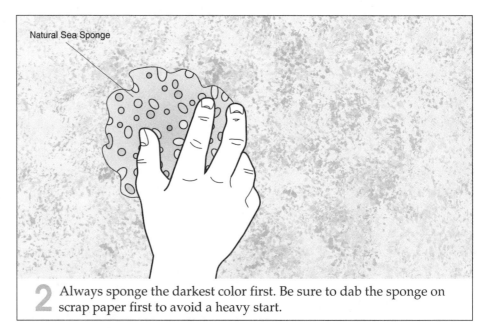

Natural Sea Sponge

2 Always sponge the darkest color first. Be sure to dab the sponge on scrap paper first to avoid a heavy start.

Sponging looks best with multiple layers of color over the base. For subtle depth use varying shades of one color over the base; for example, dark green and chrome green on light green. Or, for more vivid shading, use contrasting colors such as pink and blue over yellow base. As a rule of thumb, sponge on darkest colors first and progress to the lighter shades- this encourages depth illusion. Here's the step-by-step procedure for sponging.

1 **Mixing the Glaze.** Mix the paint with the glaze. Pour the darkest glaze mixture in the roller tray. Soak the sponge in thinner (mineral spirits for oil-based, water for water-based) and wring it almost dry. The fluid in the sponge will further soften the effect. Do not have so much liquid in the sponge that glaze runs down the surface; you want to create small droplets of color.

2 **Sponge the First Coat.** Load the darkest glaze onto the

3 Continue sponging on as many layers of color as desired. Be sure to sponge lightly and leave spaces for layers of color to show through.

sponge and dab it on scrap paper first. This will prevent a heavy start. Begin moving the sponge in vertical rows across the surface. Allow spaces for other colors; don't try to coat the surface with this color. Move your hand constantly while dabbing with your wrist and turning the sponge periodically. When you are finished clean the tray and sponge.

3 Sponge Another Coat. When the first color coating is dry and the sponge is remoistened, fill the tray with a second glaze color and begin applying it to the surface in a horizontal pattern. You should begin to see a depth illusion. Repeat with more colors if desired.

The above process uses the sponge to add glaze. For a more delicate effect you can use the sponge to remove glaze. To do this, apply the base coat, let it dry, then roll sections with glaze. Remove some of the glaze by dabbing the wall with a clean and dry sponge. Rinse and wring the sponge frequently in the appropriate thinner. You create a similar effect by rolling on thinned paint instead of glaze. Try creating patterns by moving the sponge in diagonal rows with the first color and in opposite diagonals for the second color. The beauty of decorative painting is the uniqueness of each surface so feel free to create!

Ragging

Ragging is for walls, doors, and flat surfaced furniture. The success of this finish depends on the colors in your glaze, the contrast to the base coat, and primarily upon what type of material is used to add or subtract one or more coats of glaze. A rule of thumb is: the less porous the material used, the more striking the pattern created. The most common material (for an elegant and mellow effect) is soft, clean, lint-free cotton squares. Cut these squares from old clothing or bedding, but watch for loose threads. Cheesecloth also makes a

soft pattern. More striking surfaces are made with pliable, lint-free materials such as lace, canvas or burlap.

The following method is subtractive; you'll use the rag to remove glaze. As a result you'll need two people, one to roll on a coat of glaze and the other to dab it with the rag to create the pattern. For large areas, it's best to use an oil-based glaze which will take longer to dry than a latex glaze. The longer drying time gives you more time to work. However, a latex glaze will work fine on smaller surfaces. Keep the glaze consis-

tency loose and fairly transparent for a true blended effect.

1 Rolling on the Glaze Coat. When the base coat is dry, the first person rolls the glaze on the wall in vertical strips about 3 feet wide. Apply the glaze as a thin but even coating. Too much glaze will quickly saturate the cloth and result in a muddled effect.

2 Lifting Off Glaze. Using a loosely bunched cloth moistened with paint thinner, the second person begins dabbing at the vertical column of glaze to reveal the base color and blend the glaze.

1 One person rolls on the glaze and another follows working the pattern.

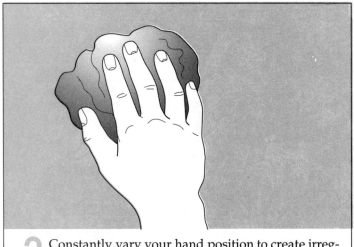

2 Constantly vary your hand position to create irregularities in the pattern.

3 Never stop the ragging process in the middle of a surface. Work to a natural stopping point.

The motion needs to be varied. Try turning your wrist various ways while moving the cloth. Dab at the wall, don't press hard. Too much pressure makes "holes" and fingerprints in the finish.

3 **Moving Down the Surface Together.** Progress in a staggered manner while always working the vertical columns of glaze into each other. As the second person finishes dabbing a row, the next row should be prepared. Always work to a natural stopping spot such as the end of a wall. Don't quit in the middle of a surface and allow the glaze to dry. Remember to wring out or change cloths when glaze is not coming off.

Rag Rolling

This technique works well for large surfaces rather than on furniture. Like ragging, rolling is a subtractive technique. The difference is, rolling produces a more formal and repetitious pattern. Work with a partner. Use oil glaze on a semi-gloss latex base color. Roll the glaze on the surface as described in Step 1 of "Ragging" process.

1 **Beginning to Roll.** Take a piece of cotton cloth about 2 feet square and loosely roll it into a cylindrical shape. Dip the roll in thinner to get it a little moist. Starting at the top of the wall roll down a row. Always roll walls in vertical columns.

2 **Overlapping the Rows.** Begin the next row by slightly overlapping the previous one. It is imperative to keep a wet edge on the columns for proper blending. Wring out or change any saturated rolls. Remember to work to a natural stop before changing rag rolls.

It is not recommended that you roll another color as the finish becomes too busy. For greater effect try a delicate ragging on of a very transparent glaze in a lighter color.

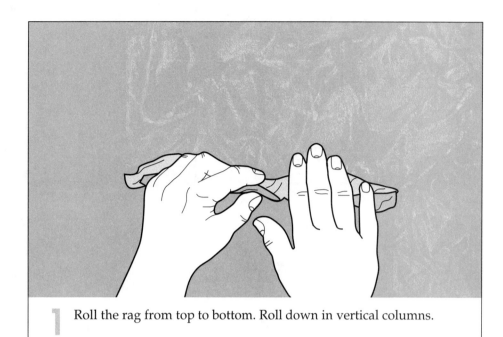

1 Roll the rag from top to bottom. Roll down in vertical columns.

2 Overlap each vertical row slightly. Keep the cloth roll loose and dry.

1 Apply an even base coat of oil-based, gloss paint.

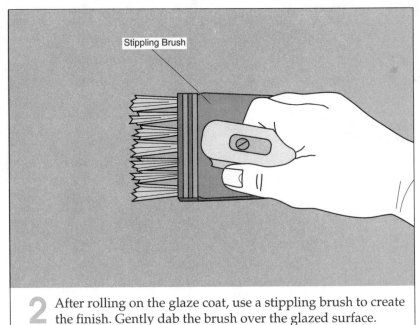

Stippling Brush

2 After rolling on the glaze coat, use a stippling brush to create the finish. Gently dab the brush over the glazed surface.

Stippling

Stippling works well for any surface, even curved molding. This finish is similar to sponging but is much more refined as the glaze is simply moved and transformed with a finely bristled stippling brush.

Stippling is more difficult than any rag technique because imperfections will show. Rag application is inherently varied but stippling makes a delicate, slightly elevated, consistent finish. The technique absolutely needs a smooth, well-prepared surface. The base coat should be an oil-based gloss and the glaze must be oil to maintain workability. Try this technique on a small surface such as a filing cabinet.

1 **Applying the Base Coat.** Carefully fill all holes and imperfections in surfaces. Prime if necessary. Apply a base coat of gloss, oil-based paint.

2 **Beginning the Stippling.** Paint the glaze on the surface in strips just ahead of your progress. A roller makes stipple-like marks naturally so use a brush only in corners. With the clean, dry bristles of the stipple brush, gently dab the brush down the row of glaze. Don't overlap the pattern created.

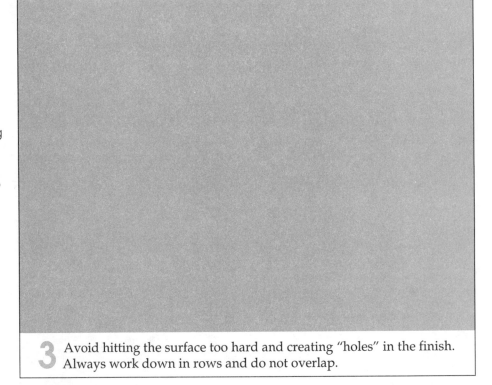

3 Avoid hitting the surface too hard and creating "holes" in the finish. Always work down in rows and do not overlap.

3 **Working the Finish.** Just touch the surface straight on so the glaze is transformed into tiny, raised droplets. If the brush doesn't hit and jump back out it will smudge the glaze and leave a blank "hole" of base color. Constantly wipe excess glaze off the bristles to avoid smudges. Complete the entire surface. Try not to go over areas twice—you'll create gaps. Also be sure to keep the bristles of the brush clean, dry and soft. For a sophisticated look, try painting bands of glaze in various shades of a color horizontally on a wall. When you stipple the wall, the colors will gently blend and change from dark at the floor to light at the top.

Dragging

Good for trim and molding, and flat surfaced furniture. Dragging produces a striped effect by pulling a dry brush in rows across a wet glaze surface. Dragging is not recommended for large, wide surfaces because it is difficult to keep the lines straight, but can be done with a plumb bob marking the vertical rows. The base coat can be oil or water-based satin paint and the glaze should be a very opaque, oil-based liquid applied in a light film. Clothing chests and cabinet doors are excellent surfaces for dragging. Try a base of a rich, deep red with an opaque white glaze dragged across.

1 **Applying the Base Coat.** Prepare the surface by filling holes and sanding or de-glossing any varnishes. Prime if necessary. Dragging emphasizes the base coat so use a satin finish and try to avoid any misses with the base color.

2 **Rolling Out the Glaze.** Begin by rolling the surface with a complete coat of glaze. Be sure to "bleed" the roller in the tray to avoid applying excessive glaze to the surface. Don't worry too much about brush marks in corners because the dragging will hide them.

3 **Pulling Down the Dragging Brush.** Pull the dragging brush across the surface in a long, straight and steady motion. Move from one end to another end. Never stop mid-point because the lines will be jagged.

4 **Keeping the Brush Clean.** Wipe bristles off before starting the next pass. Keep a wet edge between passes but don't overlap or the stripes will be too narrow at the overlap. Try to simulate the width of the bristles between vertical rows.

1 The base coat can be water or oil-based paint. Dragging works well on cabinet doors.

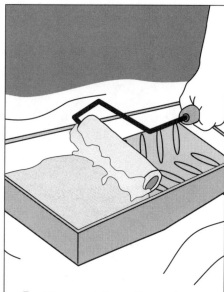

2 Bleed out the roller in the tray. Applying too much glaze will cause runs down the surface.

3 Pull the dragging brush downward in rows. Use long, straight strokes.

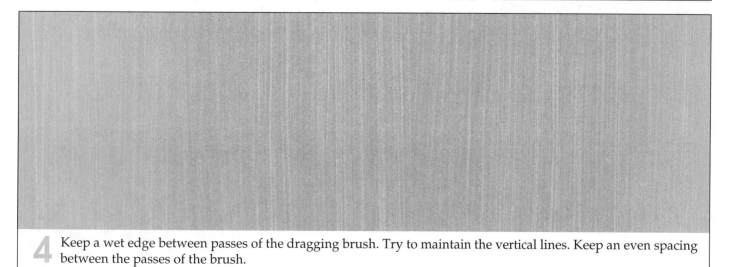

4 Keep a wet edge between passes of the dragging brush. Try to maintain the vertical lines. Keep an even spacing between the passes of the brush.

Combing

Try combing on flat, small surfaces such as the serving tray shown. This technique is similar to dragging except it creates a visually more interesting pattern. The dragging brush creates stripes that are gently blended together, whereas combing makes more distinct lines. By using different tools, some which you can make yourself, patterns are created where the glaze is lifted off. As with all the techniques, move your hand steadily to a stopping point. If you muddle an area, or stop mid-point, the surface must be reglazed and started over. Colors can be vivid to highlight pattern or similar to suggest patterns.

1 Make a Combing Tool. You can make your own tool by cutting "teeth" out of very heavy cardboard or plastic. Use a razor knife and be sure to make teeth of equal width.

2 Prepare for Combing. As with other projects you must fill any imperfections, prime the surface, and apply an even base coat to the project. When dry, brush on a coat of colored glaze.

3 Maintain the Comb Pattern. Wipe off the glaze on the comb after every pass. Follow the line of the last pass with the comb. It is important that the teeth of the comb stay fairly dry or they will just smudge the glaze.

Different Combing Pattern

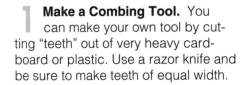

When combing there are numerous finish patterns. Here's a few of them:

■ Drag the comb in vertical rows across the entire surface then immediately comb horizontally to create a tiny boxed pattern.

■ Start at a corner of the surface and make a vertical box pattern several inches long. Pick up the comb sharply and turn it perpendicular to the first box. Make a horizontal box of the same length beside it. Repeat the vertical then horizontal pattern to create perpendicular boxes.

■ To create a striking fan pattern: Place one end of the comb in the glaze and swivel the other end around in an arc pattern. Pick the comb up and again place one end in the glaze and swivel. Repeat process over surface.

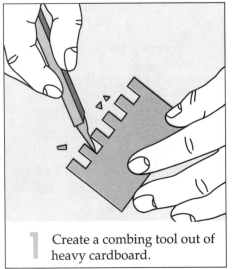

1 Create a combing tool out of heavy cardboard.

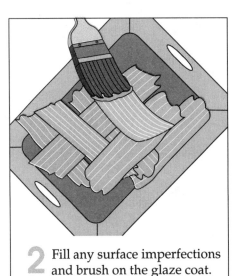

2 Fill any surface imperfections and brush on the glaze coat.

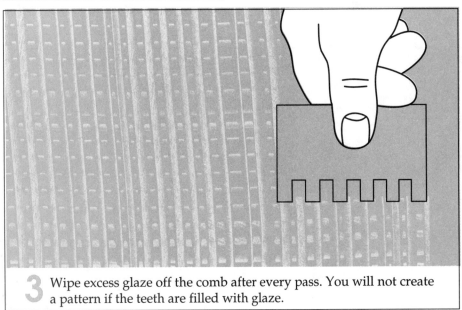

3 Wipe excess glaze off the comb after every pass. You will not create a pattern if the teeth are filled with glaze.

STORING PAINTS & PAINT EQUIPMENT

If you clean and store your tools properly, you will be able to use them for many paint jobs. Cleaning brushes, rollers and other equipment is quick and simple with the correct solvent and proper methods.

Cleaning Oil-Based Paints

Recycle the paint thinner used to clean oil-based paints. Thinner is not only expensive, it is a hazardous substance that cannot be dumped down a drain.

To clean up oil paint, you will need: Rubber gloves, eye protection (safety glasses or goggles), rags, a wire brush, at least a gallon of paint thinner, and a paint brush spinner (optional, but very useful). All of the materials are available at most paint and hardware stores.

Do not waste the time and thinner required to clean up roller covers (unless expensive lamb's wool covers were used). Leave them outside until they are completely dry, and discard them with the regular trash. Clean the roller handle using a rag soaked with paint thinner.

1 Wiping the Brush. Wear rubber gloves to protect your hands from chemicals. Use a rag to wipe off as much paint as you can from the brush and ferrule.

2 Cleaning the Paint Bucket. If you poured the paint directly into trays, find a clean, deep bucket and go to Step 3. Otherwise, pour several inches of thinner into a used paint bucket. Then, with a brush that you used for the paint job, wipe any paint off the sides and bottom of the bucket. This not only cleans the bucket, it begins the process of cleaning the brush. When the bucket is clean, pour the used thinner into any roller pans you plan to clean, and pour fresh thinner into the clean bucket. Keep a bucket for used thinner at the end of the line.

3 Using a Wire Brush. Let the brush soak in a bucket of fresh thinner for a few minutes. Then, use the wire brush to "comb" the flat sides and edges of the paintbrush from the ferrule toward the end of the bristles, forcing the paint out. Paint will be trapped inside the bristles near the ferrule, so repeat this process while dipping the brush into the thinner.

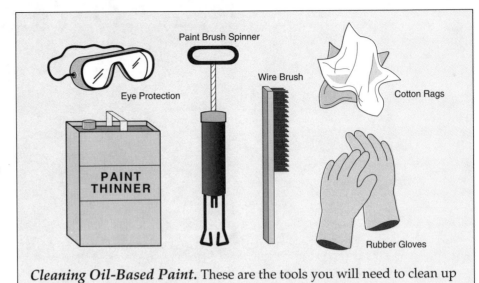

Cleaning Oil-Based Paint. These are the tools you will need to clean up a job done with oil-based paint.

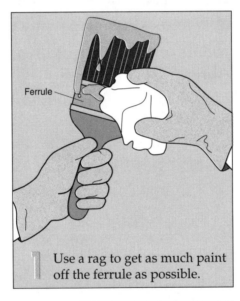

1 Use a rag to get as much paint off the ferrule as possible.

2 Use the brush to clean the sides of the bucket.

3 Use a wire brush to get paint out of the heel of the brush.

4 Use your hands to squeeze the bristles and force cleaner into the heel.

4 Forcing Thinner into Bristles. The place where the bristles meet the ferrule is called the "heel" of the brush. The heel collects paint that is tough to remove. Hold the paint brush upside-down, and bend the bristles back and forth, forcing thinner into the heel of the brush. Repeat this action several times while pouring clean thinner into the bristles. Continue until clear thinner runs out of the brush.

5 Spinning the Clean Brush. A brush spinner gets the last dregs of paint and thinner out of the brush. Place the handle of the brush into the tangs of the spinner. Hold the spinner in the paint bucket or a trash can and pump it until the brush is dry. If you do not have a spinner, spin the brush with your hands, inside the bucket or trash can.

6 Wrapping the Clean Brush. With a clean wire brush or brush comb, reshape the bristles. When the bristles are straight and parallel, wrap the clean brush in the original wrapper, or in butcher paper. This keeps the bristles from losing their shape as the brush dries. In a cool storage area, hang the brush by a hole in the handle.

Disposing of Oil-Based Paints & Solvents

Do not pour oil-based paints or thinners down the drain. Thinner and solvents in paints are hazardous materials, and dumping them down a drain ensures that they will end up in the water supply. (Yes, water goes through treatment plants in cities, but that is no excuse.)

Laws and customs for disposal of solvents are still being created.

In some areas, the local government provides local drop-off sites for such materials. Some municipalities recycle the stuff as fuel for industrial furnaces. Many municipalities tell homeowners to let paint solvents evaporate into the air, then dispose of the containers in the regular trash. Check with your local recycling agency.

7 Store the Used Thinner. Pour the used thinner (from bucket and roller trays) into a sealable container, and seal it. Let the sediment settle to the bottom. This will take a week or longer. Pour the clear thinner into a new, sealable bucket or can. Dump the sediment out onto newspaper, and let it dry thoroughly. The dry sediment, which no longer contains hazardous compounds, can be discarded with the regular trash.

Leave paint- and thinner-soaked rags outside to dry. Do not bundle and store rags; they can catch fire spontaneously! When rags are thoroughly dry, dispose of them in the regular trash.

Cleaning Water-Based Paints

The techniques for washing, combing and spinning brushes are the same for water-based paint as they are for oil-based paints. The main difference is you can work with running water in a sink or bathtub instead of buckets of solvent.

As with oil-based paint, you want to wipe as much latex paint off the brush as possible before running water over it. It is okay to wash water-thinned latex paint down the drain but you do not want to clog the drain with thick gobs of paint. Keep the water running to clear the drain

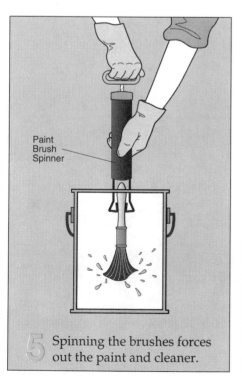

Paint Brush Spinner

5 Spinning the brushes forces out the paint and cleaner.

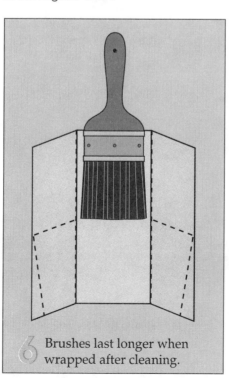

6 Brushes last longer when wrapped after cleaning.

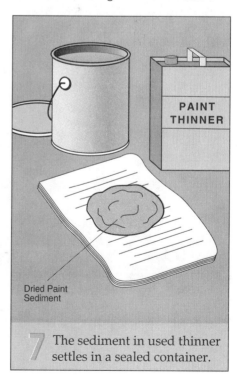

PAINT THINNER

Dried Paint Sediment

7 The sediment in used thinner settles in a sealed container.

during the cleaning process. To speed the process, add a little dish washing liquid to the water. Do the final rinse with warm water only—no soap.

Most painters do not bother to wash out a roller cover, even if the cleanup requires only soap and water. If you are using an expensive lamb's wool or mohair roller cover, it is probably worth the trouble, see page 77.

Cleaning Other Paint Products

Some coatings, such as shellac-based primers, must be cleaned up with alcohol. Lacquer must be cleaned with lacquer thinner. Working with alcohol, lacquer thinner or other solvents requires wearing rubber gloves and eye protection. Such solvents are highly flammable, be careful not to open them near pilot and other flames. Read the label directions for the right cleaning agent, and for safety precautions.

In general, it is best to use disposable brushes for shellac, as the paint dries very quickly and cleans up only with chemicals.

Caring for Brushes

Good brushes, which are necessary for a good paint job, require proper care. Here is how to get the longest life out of your brushes.

Combing the Brush

After cleaning the brush, comb the bristles with a clean wire brush or brush comb (available at most paint and hardware store). Do not tease the bristles—comb from the ferrule toward the tips of the bristles. The idea is to return the bristles to their original shape, with the bristles straight and parallel.

Wrapping the Brush

Brushes are wrapped to ensure that the bristles retain their shape as they dry. For convenience, save the stiff paper wrapper that comes with the brush. It goes on easily, and fastens in place. If you have lost the wrapper, wrap the brush in newspaper or butcher paper, and secure the paper with a rubber band.

Storing the Brush

It is best to store a brush by hanging it from the handle. Brushes can be stored flat. Do not stack or push them against other items. If the bristles are crimped or distorted during storage, they will never straighten out.

Checking the Brush

When you get ready to use the brush again, check that the bristles are soft, supple and straight—just like new. If the bristles are stiff, but can be easily broken apart, you did not get the brush quite clean enough, but it can still be used. If the bristles are stuck together and will not come apart, the brush was dirty at the time it was stored and is useless. Do not try to paint with it. If the bristles are distorted, use the brush only for non-critical applications such as applying paint remover or dusting before painting.

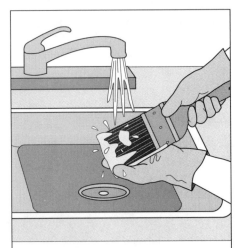

Cleaning Water-Based Paints. Rinse water-based paints off of tools under running water.

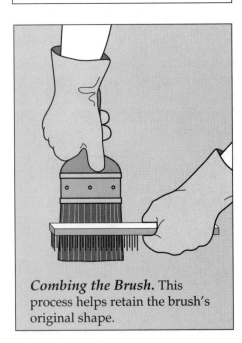

Combing the Brush. This process helps retain the brush's original shape.

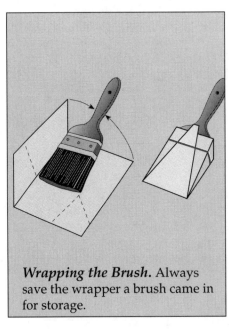

Wrapping the Brush. Always save the wrapper a brush came in for storage.

Storing the Brush. Hanging a brush helps to retain its shape.

Caring for Roller Covers

Usually, it is more trouble than it is worth to clean and store a roller cover. However, lamb's wool and mohair covers are expensive, and are designed for repeated cleaning.

Cleaning the Cover

The process for cleaning a roller cover is the same when using water or oil-based paint. Just remember to use paint thinner for oil-based products.

1 **Bleeding the Paint.** "Bleed" the paint out of the cover with a curved tool such as a five-in-one, or wring the paint out of the cover with your hands. Then hold the roller cover under warm running water (soak with clean thinner if you are using oil).

2 **Spinning out the Paint.** To clean the cover spin it with a pump spinner inside a bucket; or place the cover halfway onto a roller frame, and spin it. Repeat Step 1 until runoff from the cover is clear and clean.

3 **Wrapping the Cover.** Store the roller cover on end until it is completely dry. Try to let the cover dry without anything pressed against it as this may cause depressions in the nap. When the cover is completely dry, store it in the original plastic wrapper, or wrap it in newspaper or butcher paper.

Caring for Other Tools

Roller pans, scrapers, putty knives and all other painting tools are cleaned with water or the appropriate solvent, then stored in a cool, dry place. Why a cool, dry place? Because metal parts rust when stored in hot, humid areas. Make sure all tools are thoroughly dry before storing them. Wet spots tend to rust during storage. To guard against rust, apply a thin coating of oil or WD-40.

Curved Painter's Tool

1 Work the paint out of the roller cover with a five-in-one tool or wring it by hand.

2 Finish cleaning the cover by spinning it and forcing paint and solvent out.

3 Do not allow anything to lean against the cover as it dries.

When you retrieve the tools for the next paint job, check for rust. Do not use a roller pan that has rust in places that contact the roller cover. Other tools can be lightly sanded to remove rust. If the tools were coated with oil before storage, wipe them down with mineral spirits to remove oil before using them again.

Cleaning Drips & Spills

If you get a drop of oil-based paint on a smooth finished surface, it is best to let the paint dry, then pop the paint off with a razor blade. Drips of latex paint can be wiped up while still wet. Use a damp cloth. If you find dried drips of latex, use a proprietary solvent such as Goof-Off.

If you spill a significant amount of paint on carpet or upholstery, call a professional carpet and upholstery cleaner. There is a chance the fabric can be saved. Very small drips often can be shaved off the carpet with a razor blade.

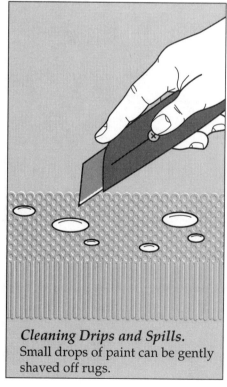

Cleaning Drips and Spills. Small drops of paint can be gently shaved off rugs.

Storing Paint

Flammable solvents are best stored in a locked metal cabinet, preferably in an outbuilding. Do not store flammable materials in an area where there is a chance fumes could be ignited by the pilot flame of a water heater or furnace.

Keeping Paint On Hand

After the job is finished, keep some paint on hand for touch-ups, and for matching the paint in future paint jobs. Keep the paint labels—if colors are discontinued, a paint store often can match paints from the information on the label. If only a small amount of paint is left in a can, it will likely dry out. Pour the paint into a smaller container. Paint stores might have quart cans available; if not, a glass jar, suitable for canning vegetables, does the job.

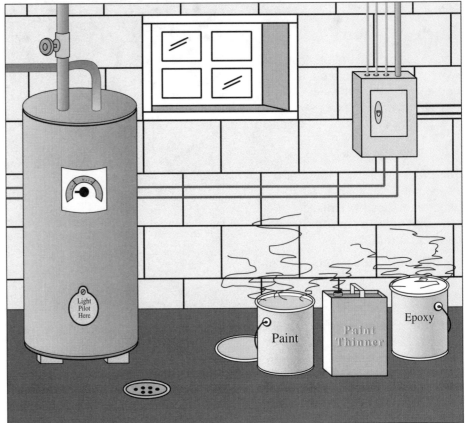

Storing Paint. Never store flammable solvents near appliances with pilot flames as the fumes can ignite.

Keeping Paint on Hand. Small amounts of leftover paint can be sealed in jars to keep them workable for touch-ups and matching.

Storing Paint Cans

If the rim of the can is clogged with dried paint, dig it out with an old screwdriver. Do not worry if some dried paint falls into the can; just strain the paint before you use it.

Place the lid on the can, then cover the lid with newspaper or a piece of cloth (this prevents splashing). Tap the lid into place with a rubber mallet. If you do not have a rubber mallet, tap lightly with a hammer. Tap all the way around the lid, while listening to the sound. When the taps sound the same all the way around, the lid is firmly in place.

Store latex paint where it will not freeze. If latex paint freezes, it is useless. In this case, open the can, let it dry out, and discard the remaining paint.

Storing Paint Cans. Covering a paint lid before closing it prevents spattering from the lip.

Alligatoring Paint failure condition where the paint pulls apart in a crazed line pattern resembling alligator skin. Caused by paint applied too thickly; paint that dried too quickly; or a second coat painted over a first coat that was not dry.

Base Coat In decorative painting this is the solid color of either gloss or semi-gloss paint that shows underneath the glaze coat pattern.

Blistering Paint problem characterized by paint coming off the surface in bubbles. Caused by paint applied over a wet, oily or dirty surface. Also occurs when water vapor escapes from the house interior.

Caulk A soft compound for sealing joints and cracks against leaks of water and air. It may be silicone, or a latex synthetic compound.

Chalking Paint failure marked by a layer of fine dust on the surface of the paint. Occurs with time as weather conditions break down the paint film.

Chemical stripper A paint removing agent. Usually applied with a brush but may be embedded in a plastic-covered poultice that is laid on a surface then pulled off.

Combing A decorative painting technique using a comb of varying teeth width dragged across a glazed surface.

Compressed air sprayer An electric sprayer that emits a fine mist of paint by forcing air through a paint reservoir.

Decorative painting Paint process in which a semi-transparent glaze color is manipulated to create a pattern which highlights a solid base color underneath.

Dragging Creating a lined pattern in a glaze coat by pulling a brush with long bristles in overlapping vertical rows

Drywall Also known as wallboard, gypsum board, and plasterboard; a paper-covered sandwich of gypsum plaster used for wall and ceiling construction.

Epoxy A two-part compound used to fill holes in damaged wood. Once dry, epoxy patches are very strong and can be sanded, primed, and painted.

Ferrous metal primer Specially formulated primer applied to iron-bearing metal. Commonly needed for gutters and flashing.

Flashing A shiny spotting effect in paint sheen caused by applying wet paint over an area of dry paint.

Foam brush An 1- to 4-inch, taper-edged foam pad on a stick for applying stain and painting window muntins.

Glaze Opaque, gel-like "paint" used for decorative painting, can be water- or oil-based.

Ladder jack A plank-scaffold support arm resembling a shelf bracket. A pair of these arms (usually made of aluminum) attach to the rungs of two ladders to support an aluminum plank-scaffold.

Latex paint Paint that uses water as the vehicle to spread on, and adhere to a surface. Comes in all sheens (flat to high gloss enamel). Favored for quick drying time, easy water clean-up, and environmental safety.

Methylene chloride A chemical compound thought to be carcinogenic. Contained in most effective chemical strippers.

Muntins Strips that separate window panes. On older windows muntins hold glass in place; on newer windows they are decorative.

Natural bristles Also called "China bristles". Brush bristles from animal hair (usually hog). Use this type for oil-based paint only.

Oil paint Type of paint that uses either natural oil (such as linseed oil) or a synthetic oil (called alkyd) as the spreading and adhering vehicle. Alkyd paints are the most prevalent oil paint. Oil-based paint requires mineral spirits or turpentine to clean and thin.

Palm sander A small, electric sander with vibrating pad to which sandpaper is clamped. Shaped to fit a palm, this tool facilitates woodwork sanding.

Peeling Paint failure where paint falls off the surface. Peeling is caused by moisture problems and expansion of the painted surface.

Power roller A device that pumps paint either directly from a can or from an integrated reservoir into a roller cover. Eliminates the need to continually reload a roller cover when rolling a surface.

Primer An essential undercoat layer of paint. Primer kills stains, retards moisture absorption, and provides a good surface for a top coat of paint to adhere. Primer comes in water- and oil-based formulas. It is imperative that new or bare wood, and metal, be primed.

Propulsion sprayer Machine that spits or "flips" small droplets of paint. Paint is supplied by either an attached reservoir or drawn from a paint can. With adjustable rate of spray mist and pressure these machines are excellent for spraying large surfaces.

Rag rolling Process of rolling a loosely wound rag down a glazed surface in vertical columns. Creates a soft, repetitive pattern.

Ragging Decorative paint process using a bunched-up rag to remove glaze and create a mottled pattern with the underneath base color.

Roller cover Cylindrical cover used over a roller handle to roll paint onto a surface. Available in varying nap thickness for specific tasks and made of either nylon, lamb's wool or foam.

Rotary disk sander Hand-held machine to which an abrasive sanding disk is attached to remove large areas of paint on flat surfaces.

Rough-surface painter A combination brush and paint pad, this tool is useful for painting rough shingles and masonry. Short bristles resemble a scrub brush.

Sash Brush A finely bristled brush with an angled taper that makes sharp lines on trim, molding and window muntins.

Sash The framework into which window glass is set. Double-hung windows have an upper and lower sash.

Scaffolding Connected metal sections with lumber planks, or an aluminum plank spanning two ladder jacks used as an elevated work platform.

Sheen The degree of gloss in a paint. Sheen ranges from flat to high gloss.

Sponging The use of a natural sea sponge, or synthetic sponge with ripped edges, dipped in colored glaze to apply decorative finish on a solid base coat.

Stain brush A short and wide bristled brush used for stain. The bristles reduce the amount of stain that runs into the brush ferrule.

Stippling Process of gently removing a glaze coat with the fine bristles of a stippling brush.

Trisodium phosphate (TSP) A strong, low-sud, powdered cleaning agent to be mixed with water and used to clean house exteriors and walls that have remaining wallpaper glue.